Artisanal Cheesemaking

First published 2007
© John Knox Limited

John Knox Limited
Glenmore House, 55 Rose Bank,
Leek, Staffordshire ST13 6AG
Tel. 01538 399733
email: john@johnknoxltd.co.uk
www.johnknoxltd.co.uk

ISBN 978-0-9555245-0-9

Designed and typeset by
David Cliffe Associates, Leek Tel. 01538 398896

Printed by
JH Brookes (Printers) Ltd, Stoke on Trent

Artisanal Cheesemaking

A comprehensive guide to cheesemaking
methods and recipes, establishing and
operating a cheesemaking plant, and
marketing the finished product

John Knox

M.Sc., C.Sci., F.C.M.I., M.C.Q.I., F.I.F.S.T

Contents

Illustrations and charts

Acknowledgements

- My wife Margaret for her encouragement and typing most of my original book.

- Max King of Business Link, a friend and helper during the various stages of my cheese business development.

- David Salt of Leek, for considerable help with data and photographs in Chapter 2.

- Karen Davies, MBE, Chris Bonds and Debbie Coxon of Heart of England Fine Foods, for their continuous encouragement and help with our marketing efforts.

- Brian Goddard, Ian Kiley and Sandra Butterworth of the Business Innovation Centre, Stafford, for arranging our first cheesemaking premises and also helping us to get a development grant.

- Staffordshire Moorlands District Council for providing small financial grants which had a disproportionate effect on raising our morale, especially after the Foot and Mouth crisis. The price weight labeller was a tremendous boon to our small business.

- Sheila Penfold at "A Taste of Staffordshire", for marketing and sales assistance.

- Juliet Harbutt of "The British Cheeses Awards", for great marketing opportunities.

- Suzanne Banker, Silverstone, for enabling us to acquire and develop our second cheese dairy at Cheddleton.

- Sue Talks for typing Chapter 7 of this book.

- Staffordshire Moorlands District Council, Environmental Health Department, for their support and direction, to Chris Hampton and especially our designated E.H.O. Ian Stewart.

- DEFRA, London, Simon Johnson and his staff, especially Funda Lancaster, for their help and support in the preparation of the PDO (Place of Designated Origin) for the Staffordshire Cheese.

- PKF, Acccountants and Business Advisors, Stoke on Trent, for translating my market research, product sales vloumes, costs and margins into a professional financial format for Chapter 7.

- Finally my editor David Cliffe for his imaginative approach to setting out my text and data.

CHAPTER ONE

Revival of a Moorlands Tradition

 **The life-changing decision that turned a dream of cheesemaking in the Moorlands into a thriving business with award-winning products and a host of new friends.**

I had a dream.... To re-introduce cheesemaking in the Staffordshire Moorlands and create Staffordshire's own cheese brand. That dream became a reality with the success of the Staffordshire Cheese company – a long way from my humble introduction to the world of cheese four decades earlier.

I had become interested in milk when still at grammar school in Glasgow – I started delivering the stuff for the local Co-op when I was 16. Someone told me that they made cheese from milk and at the age of 17 I took off for six weeks' school holidays to the Scottish Milk Marketing Board cheese factory at Mauchline in Ayrshire, to wash cheese vats, scrub floors and taste some of the most amazing Cheddar and Dunlop cheese made in the world.

I soon learned just how precious their cheeses were. One day I was asked to carry one of the cloth-bound 12 kilo round cheeses to the store. Passing the cheesemaker by the vat, his tender words were the unforgettable "If you're going to fall son, make sure it's on your back, so that you don't damage *my* cheese."

After studying science I joined the dairy industry and went on to work for some of the biggest names in the UK business, leading to 14 years as manufacturing director with a large dairy company based in the Staffordshire Moorlands. Life was to take a new turn, however. In October 1989 I was made redundant. What was I to do? Well, after devoting myself and my energies to a large concern for so long, I decided I could no longer carry on with that way of life for two main reasons:

1. The popularity of manufacturing plant rationalisations meant I would probably be made redundant again.

2. Hundreds of decent, hard working, devoted shop-floor staff had also lost their jobs and I did not want to spend my life making the people who were "the salt of the earth" redundant.

I discussed the dilemma with my wife, Margaret, who advised me to go into food manufacturing. I was a bit more cautious and suggested consultancy. She was not too impressed by the idea – as she had met many consultants in her role as a Personnel

Manager in a large textile company – but I prepared a five-year plan and started. This was a time when major focus was being put on Quality Systems. The food industry had always been good at Quality Control but not Quality Assurance, i.e. problem prevention. My unique selling point was that I could help manufacturers develop their business management as well as quality.

In the next five years I took my M.Sc. degree at the University of Birmingham, Edgbaston and also became a professionally qualified quality assurance consultant and training centre for quality systems auditors. However, I still hankered after doing something in cheese manufacture. In the sixth year of my "self-employment" (the consultancy was now a limited company and employed four consultants and an administrator). I took the plunge and decided to experiment with cheesemaking. Margaret was happy for me to do this, but reminded me "I want nothing to do with cheese or cheese sales or packing or anything!"

Our first "laboratory"

During the first year I continued with consultancy but rented a 500 sq ft "laboratory" at Knutton, Newcastle-under-Lyme from the Staffordshire Business Innovation Centre. Brian Goddard, Ian Kiley and Sandra Butterworth of the Innovation Centre were great people and I reciprocated by giving talks and taking part in their business presentations. At the "laboratory" my daughter Fiona and her friend Maggie Hartley helped me carry out my trials with different cheese cultures and types of cheeses. We also rented the cheese room at Reaseheath College and Express Dairies at Malpas, Cheshire. Sometimes we hired in extra cheesemakers' help but the hired cheesemakers sometimes found our developments frustrating for some reason! One particular helper who was very skilled used to throw cheese equipment around the room. We never knew why, but it did have us "crying with laughter." Thankfully the equipment was not our own, it was part of the hire arrangement!

During this trial period I started developing some sales and giving talks at village halls, business centres, dinners, charity functions and the like. The cheese business was taking on a life of its own and I was getting carried away with enthusiasm and interest in all things cheese!

After a year my dear friends at the Business Innovation Centre helped me gain a £20,000 investment grant which I matched with £20,000. I had sent our first cheese, Archie's Choice, to the Bakewell Show – it gained first prize in its category – wow! It was now time to develop a larger facility and appropriate equipment. We eventually moved to a 2,500 square foot factory.

Fiona and Maggie were now trained cheesemakers and my son Simon decided to come and help us also. Artisanal cheesemaking equipment was not available off-the-shelf and so I had to design and have my equipment made by local engineers.

Fiona loved this development period and gave all of the pieces of equipment names. The cheese milling machine was "Millie". We had a food grade plastic rake for stirring the milk, if Simon used it (he is 6'3") it was called "The Big Stirrer" and if I used it (I am 5'7½", remember the ½), it was called the "Little Stirrer". The cheesepress was "Jess", the pasteuriser "Percy", the tank was "Frank" and the cheese vat "Vi"!

We made the cheese to classical music, which could be quite difficult if someone played a rousing piece of music during the cutting of the coagulum when we had to be particularly slow and gentle.

Our milk arrived the day before cheesemaking and Simon would make sure that the raw milk tank was clean and sterile ready for the "white stuff". Simon always checked the levels in the tank when the bulk milk tanker driver was finished. On one memorable occasion he called a 6'6" giant to account as there was about an inch less milk in our tank when he shouted "finished"!

After about a year Fiona had got carried away with computers and started studying for a degree (she got a 1st Class Honours in Applied Computers by 2006) and so left us to study and teach. Maggie got fired up also and went to start her own business, leaving Simon and I to carry on. We still needed help and thankfully my wife came to the rescue. Despite her original determination not to get involved, she was soon expert at cheese cutting and packing, not to mention waxing. On one occasion whilst waxing a 2kg half round of Archie's Choice, she dropped the cheese into the waxing bath with an explosion of hot wax firing out of the bath, and over Margaret, the walls and the floor!

Sales had to be developed and I was out there to spread the word for our products. The NEC, London Food Show, Heart of England Fine Foods (HEFF) events, the British Cheese Awards, local fine foods events and the 'Taste of Staffordshire' awards all raised our profile and at the same time we met lots of people who wanted to help, Karen and Chris (HEFF), Juliet Harbutt (British Cheese Awards), Sheila Penfold (Taste of Staffordshire) and many others.

Farmers' markets – friendly havens of fine food

Farmers' markets became an important focus and here we met many dedicated artisans who, like us, were producing local foods from local ingredients. They were a band of enthusiasts who wanted to produce food "the way it used to be" – handmade, no additives, only fresh raw materials straight from the local land. What an experience.

We went to markets at **Bakewell** (always a well run and great sales market); **Sheffield** (incredible Christmas sales); **Stafford** (good steady clientele); **Buxton** (oh so cold in open market place, but considerable sales at "The Great Peak District Fair" held in the Octagon, Pavilion Gardens); **Nottingham** (we were always watching our cash box); **Mansfield** (steady but not great sales); **Lichfield** (a good market with regular customers particularly for our smoked cheese); **Penkridge** (hard work but good sales); **Newcastle-under-Lyme** (fantastic service to stallholders and great sales, especially at Christmas); **Sutton Coldfield** (market in the middle of town, very good as a people watching venue, but sales were barely acceptable); **Ashbourne** (this market never really took off and stopped after one season); **Uttoxeter** (a successful market for a short period until a farmers' market shop opened); **Stone** (venue for the first Staffordshire farmers' market. A great success for about 18 months, then disappeared to reappear about seven years later as a successful monthly event); **Derby** (badly organised) **Long Eaton** and **Ilkeston** (fair markets to attend); **Loughborough** (a good market to start with then the organisers allowed non-producers to come with "bought-in" items, especially re-sale cheese, it became non-viable for us); **Nantwich** (reasonable sales, great position in the middle of town, we stopped going as the number of markets in Staffordshire increased); **Belper** (great position, great organisation and great sales. A very enjoyable market where we had many interesting customers); **Ripley** (as cold as Buxton. Sales were fair and the stallholders' repartee unforgettable); **Hartington** (held on Hartington Moor every Sunday in summer – great fun and great bonhomie among stallholders); **Heanor** (not too successful and "crashed" after a few months); Hinckley (reasonable sales); **Congleton** (hopeless sales, attended only one market); **Vale Royal** (held at Eddisbury Fruit Farm, Kelsall. Sales reasonable and a great atmosphere among customers and stallholders).

At these markets we met many great producers who became great friends:

Halfpenny Green, Martin Vickers, Clive and Lisa (tel. 01384 221122). Red, white, rosé, Champagne-type English sparkling white and rosé wine.

Cocodance, Bridget Joyce and Dave Golubows (tel. 01433 6211334). Chocolates par excellence. An amazing range of chocolate types and shapes.

Jag Crafts, Judith Wood (tel. 01538 266337). Wood carvings and wooden gifts covering a considerable range of items.

Port of Lancaster Smoke House, Michael Price (tel. 01524 751493). Smoker of fish, chicken, cheese. The chicken was 'to die for'.

Field House Foods, Steve Croot (tel. 01332 883072). Steve prepares flavoured oils and vinegars. Especially the garlic oils and white Balsamic vinegar. All of his products are good enough to drink.

The Original Farmers Market Shop, Bakewell, Richard Young and Carolyn Fisher (tel. 01629 815814). Richard started this shop and gave a very welcome boost to the sale of many artisanal products.

Oslinc, Boston, Lincs (tel. 01507 568885). Ostrich fillets and steaks. Best served rare to medium rate. Fry in a little oil, quickly sealing the meat each side, then cook for two to three minutes each side before serving. Ostrich burgers with onions and mustard – "heaven!". Ostrich looks and tastes like beef, but is lower in fat than chicken or turkey.

Yabba, Stephanie Brown (tel. 0114 275 6066). Cooking sauces, chutneys, dressings, marinades and pickles. A great enthusiast.

Truly Scrumptious, Jim and Christine Grayson (tel. 01246 567735). Some sugar-free, gluten-free, but mainly traditional hand made yummy cakes. The most amazing Bakewell tart made with all ground almonds. Carrot cake bursting with real carrots and walnuts. Indulgent chocolate brownies which sell within the hour.

Peter Storey, Ashbourne (tel. 01335 300059). Rare breed meats, sausages and bacon. You can also stay at the farm where you can see the animals and have amazing bed and breakfast.

New Close Farm, Over Haddon, Bakewell, Jim and Jane Armstrong (tel. 01629 814280). Rare breeds pork and bacon. Farm shop, but at the market you have to be quick as the main cuts of meat are sold within the hour.

Margaret was now into some markets but after an exceptionally cold market at Buxton, she had to sit in the car for 30 minutes with the heating on before she could drive home, her marketing days were finished!

We got involved in many presentations and promotions. For example, at Foxt village hall in the Stafforshire Moorlands, I gave a 30-minute cheese presentation and was bombarded with an hour of interesting questions. It was here that I met one of the Moorlands' great farming characters, Mrs Christine Chester, who gave me the recipe for cheesemaking at Townhead Farm, Foxt from the 18th Century. I re-created this cheese and won a Bronze Medal at the British Cheese Awards.

We had many memorable occasions, but none more so than 15 November 1999 when we met Prince Charles at Highgrove. This was to celebrate the tenth anniversary of the Specialist Cheesemakers' Association. The Prince was charming and very supportive. Awaiting his arrival many cheesemakers were up around what appeared to be the main entrance to the room. He actually entered the room through a disguised door in the back wall and walked straight into Margaret who soon had him guffawing with laughter. It was a wonderful evening of excellent cheeses, excellent wine and excellent company.

Some of those who supported us

Over our time spent developing the Staffordshire Cheese many characters came to work for us. We had to find people who would work well and have a sense of humour – you needed one! These sterling workers included:

Colleen Birchall (Leek) – cheese

Katie Ridge (Leek) – cheese and markets

Angela Ferns(Leek) – cheese and markets

Margaret Hartley (Cheddleton) – cheese and markets

Fiona Knox(Uttoxeter) – cheese and markets

Diane Howard (Leek) – cheese and markets

David Howard (Hartington) – cheese and markets

Ray Walmsley (Leek) – market sales

Alison McRobbie (Newcastle) – markets

Anne Jones (Yorkshire) – markets

Alison Bould (Leek) – markets

Charles Pickford (Moorlands) – cheese and markets

Pat Fernandez (Moorlands) – cheese and markets

In all the cheese activities my son Simon was always the main man. Devoted, focussed, enthusiastic, he carried out his cheesemaking, cleaning and sterilising duties with the preciseness of a brain surgeon! He was always thinking ahead and commenting on how we did things. Always looking for improvements.

In 2004 I launched the Staffordshire Cheese at the Stafford Show and started down a path to achieve Place of Designated Origin (PDO) for this remarkable product. It had been made on many Moorlands' farms in the 18th and 19th Centuries but totally disappeared around 1945.

During all of these times my grandchildren, Liberty, Imogen and Henry would have some involvement in the cheese packing activities, especially when we used to weigh cheeses and prepare the labels by hand which also meant manually calculating the price. Our young workers were adept at these activities and worked as an effective team on those days when no cheesemaking activities were taking place. My other grandchildren, Madeline, Jude, Sam and Louis, were too young at this stage, but perhaps in the future they will have some involvement in cheese!

Staffordshire Moorlands District Council were another source of encouragement to us, especially in helping us to recover from the effects of Foot and Mouth crisis in 2001 and also giving small grants to enable us to buy an automatic price labelling machine. What a boon that was to the business.

Working practices

The outside cold store was an important part of our process. Cheeses were held here at 10°C for many months of maturation. It was also a focus for local young people who seemed to treat it as the ultimate challenge – "What's in there and how do we break the door down?" On many occasions we found evidence of trying to saw through padlocks or crowbar the door open, but fortunately they never succeeded.

Inside the factory we had to modify the building for food requirements. The breeze block walls were given three coats of an anti-bacterial paint, which completely sealed the blocks and also made the walls easy to clean. We put a 6mm U-crete expoxy floor on top of the standard concrete and angled the floor to the drains. This was extremely important to ensure satisfactory drainage and no waste liquid "pockets" in the floor area. U-crete is a chemical resistant screed; its durable surface provides a slip resistant finish, which complies with health and safety executive requirements. Our light fittings were a large halogen design with shatterproof protection.

Infestation control was another priority and the "mouseman" would come every month to do his checks, replenish whatever and give us his stories of fishing and hunting.

All equipment was of stainless steel design and, as described earlier, key pieces of plant were named by my daughter Fiona. With the cheese room we had a large cold store (0-4°C) for storing our packed sales cheese. The production flow started at the stainless steel raw milk tank, then to the electronic pasteuriser, the 2000L cheese vat. The salted curds were packed into muslin cloth lined stainless steel cheese mould (10Kg) or 5Kg white food grade plastic moulds for pressing in the vertical hand operated press or horizontal air press. These moulds gave either traditional cloth bound cheeses or rindless cheeses.

Because we wanted to give a direct service to our customers and not work through middle men, we controlled all our own cheese sales. If we had looked to the next level of selling, then we would have considered going to selected cheesemongers or cheese factors as well as selected major retailers and regional food groups.

In the event we sold mainly through the farmers' markets and our weekly sales run around Staffordshire. Our customers kindly took a month's cheese supply allowing us flexibility to expand our deliveries. Some customers who helped our development were:

Andrew and Janet Bould (butchers) of Leek who gave us much
encouragement and sales
John and Dawn Broadhurst, cheese sellers at the Buttermarket, Leek
Peter Coates (butchers) of Alrewas
Clunie at Churasco's restaurant in Hanley

The Bakewell Farmers' Market Shop run by Richard

Byrkley Park Garden Centre

Carsington Water shop

Patrick and Brooksbank of Ashbourne (they gave me my first cheese order)

Marie at the fabulous Burnt Gate Pub in Burton-on-Trent

Country Fruit Store in Stafford

The Hartington Cheese Shop

The marvellous Three Horseshoes Inn at Blackshaw Moor, near Leek

Essington Farm were great supporters of our cheeses

Johnsons of Yoxall (butchers and delicatessen)

David and Carol Wheat of Cheadle bought considerable Christmas cheeses to sell on their milk round

Pam at Beech Farm Shop

Buxton Pavilion

Fine Feathers Farm at Endon

The Yew Tree Inn, Ranton, Stafford

Abbey Executive Wines sold good volumes at Christmas as did the Titanic Brewery and our dear friend Francis Peel and his staff at Whitebridge Wines of Stone who bought many Christmas Truckles.

These are only some of the customers who gave us support and encouragement in our efforts.

How the business grew

During all of these cheese activities I still did some consultancy, my wife typed my consultancy reports and a friend from Newcastle-under-Lyme came monthly for a two-hour chat. He was my mentor and had been a successful company chairman. On many occasions we met at a club or restaurant and following the meeting our wives joined us for lots of food and wines!

Our Archie's Choice cheese was named after our grandson Archie Knox Chapman who died at 17 months of age from brain tumour. We were all devastated and then my mother-in-law died throwing us all into deeper despair. Like all tragedies we gradually recovered and were amused when my wife's step-father married for the fourth time at 92 years of age. His new wife was 76. He died a year later!

Things at home also improved. We had our half-acre hillside garden terraced into eight bush gardens – as a magical a place for our seven grandchildren as it had been for our own children.

Rick Stein, the TV chef and restaurateur, discovered our cheeses in 2002 and made us one of his "Food Heroes" featured in his BBC TV series on Britain's artisanal food manufacturers. Rick believes that "mass-produced food often extracts a high price on the environment, on rural economies, on the survival of traditional cultures and skills." Many of the producers featured in his 'Guide to the Food Heroes of Britain' (published by BBC) address these problems, "painstakingly maintaining traditional methods, passing them on through their families and staff, when a modern approach would certainly be more profitable".

The business continued to grow and production from our factory reached a quarter of a tonne of cheese a day in twelve varieties including:

The Staffordshire: A handmade cloth bound vegetarian cheese made from cows' milk.

Archie's Choice: Made from pasteurised Staffordshire cows' milk with added cream vegetarian rennet and a selection of cultures for acid and flavour. It has a creamy, crumbly texture and rounded, slightly tangy flavour. Won a Bronze Medal at British Cheese Awards.

Archie's Traditional: A cloth bound cheese with a 'creamy' sensation on the palate and a distinct fresh flavour.

Moorlander – Oak Smoked: Based on the Archie's Choice recipe and smoked over burning oak wood to give a delicate smoked flavour.

Captain Smith's Titanic: In this cheese the warm curds are washed in Captain Smith's Real Ale from the Titanic Brewery of Burslem, Stoke on Trent. The cheese is moist with an initial tangy flavour with the subtle taste of hopes coming through at the end.

The Abbey Beer and Garlic: A traditional cloth bound cheese which has a subtle flavour of hops and a lingering flavour of garlic. Winner of a Silver Medal at the British Cheese Awards.

Cheddleton – with Additives: These cheeses have either chives or cranberries.

Dream of Abbey: A semi-soft cheese which has a dense texture, fresh flavour and smooth finish.

Foxt: Based on the cheese making in the village of Foxt, Staffordshire in 1860. Similar to Gouda in texture and with a distinctive rich flavour. Winner of a Bronze Medal at the British Cheese Awards.

Soft and Hard Goats' Cheese: Both use Staffordshire goats' milk, the soft cheese has a white mould and the hard cheese has a slightly crumbly texture. This latter cheese won a Bronze Medal at the British Cheese Awards.

At the same time I kept promoting our cheeses, continuing to go to national and local food events, giving cheese talks at many venues. Simon was "solid as a rock" in helping with the preparation for farmers' markets. It took about two hours to arrange the cheese and ancillary equipment for a market and when I returned it took at least two more hours to check stocks and wash equipment. He handled all of this without fuss or problem.

In late 2004 I had been on a Leicestershire farm with my friend Haroon Shaikh. We came back into Leicester for a coffee and sandwich. After leaving the café we were walking along a flat stretch of road when I suddenly went breathless, collapsed and woke up several minutes later on the pavement with Haroon cradling my head and calling on his mobile for an ambulance. Within an hour I had been well tested and located in a hospital ward. Haroon met up with my other friend Malcolm Rossa and they set off for Leek to return my car, fetch Margaret and take her to a hotel.

It was the beginning of the end of my cheesemaking. As I recovered from major heart surgery for heart failure – a new aortic valve and double by-pass – we sold the company as a going concern to Adrian Corke and Sue Carline, local artisan beer brewers. But cheese remains an important part of life as I develop my consultancy again and encourage farmers to make Staffordshire cheeses.

CHAPTER TWO

History of Cheesemaking
on the Staffordshire-Derbyshire borders

 **Brought to the moorland district by 13th Century monks, cheesemaking grew into a thriving farmhouse activity followed by the establishment of many village factories.**

The re-introduction of cheesemaking to the Staffordshire Moorlands revived a craft with a long and proud heritage in the area. With a history stretching back the best part of a thousand years, cheese making in the rural districts of the Staffordshire-Derbyshire borders was once a thriving activity with recipes and skills passed down through generations of local farmers.

The history of cheese itself stretches back much further – right back to the early days of civilisation. Archaeologists have discovered that as far back as 6000BC cheese had been made from cow and goats' milk and stored in tall jars. Egyptian tomb murals of 2000BC show butter and cheese being made, and other murals which show milk being stored in skin bags suspended from poles demonstrate a knowledge of dairy husbandry at that time.

It is likely that Nordic tribes of Central Asia found animal skin bags a useful way to carry milk on animal backs when on the move. Fermentation of the milk sugars would cause the milk to curdle and the swaying motion would break up the curd to provide a refreshing whey drink. The curds would then be removed, drained and slightly salted to provide a tasty and nourishing high protein food.

The Romans significantly developed the art of cheesemaking. In the fertile lowlands of Europe dairy husbandry developed at a faster pace and cheesemaking from cow's milk became the norm. Hence, the particular development of cheeses such as Edam and Gouda in the Netherlands. This was much copied elsewhere. A hard pressed cheese, relatively small in size, brine-salted and waxed to reduce moisture losses during storage, proved both marketable and easy to distribute.

Some cheese varieties with date first recorded:

Gorgonzola	879AD	Parmesan	1579
Roquefort	1070	Stilton	1785
Cheddar	1500	Camembert	1791

Cheesemaking comes to the Moorlands

Cheesemaking was significantly developed in the British Isles by Cistercian monks after the Norman Conquest and monks were in fact some of the earliest cheese makers in the Staffordshire Moorlands. It was a group from the same religious order, led by their abbot, Richard of Poulton, who arrived on the outskirts of the Manor of Leek in April of the year 1214. The monks, who founded Dieulacres Abbey near the River Churnet about half a mile north of the town, were sheep farmers and produced significant amounts of wool. They were vegetarian, self-sufficient and part of their diet was cheese. The Rev. Michael J Fisher (author of 'Dieulacres Abbey, Leek') confirms that at the dissolution of the monastery in October 1539 there were two wooden cheese tubs and a brining bath for the cheese.

Leek had been granted its Market Charter by King John as early as 1207 and over subsequent centuries it became an important market centre for the surrounding rural area.

By the year 1607 we learn that *"Leek is said to have had a good weekly market, which is now held every Wednesday, and is well supplied with all kinds of provisions, exposed for sale in the spacious market place, which occupies the most central and highest part of the town and has several good streets branching from it in several directions... Cheese fairs were established here about ten years ago (1597), and are now held three times a year on the second Monday in March, and the third Mondays in September and November."*

(The Victorian history of Stafford Vol. VII Leek and the Moorlands. Published by Oxford University Press)

Markets and fairs held in the township of Longnor were also important over a long period and as early as 1478 there was a November fair for the sale of cheese.

The agricultural setting

An insight into the diet of poor people and agricultural conditions in the Moorlands during the 18th Century comes from 'General View of the Agriculture of the County of Stafford' by W. Pitt of Pendeford, nr. Wolverhampton. Published in 1796.

"I have travelled through most of our kingdom, and find the lower classes of people vary much in their manner of living," Pitt states.

"In the North of England their chief diet is bread and milk, perhaps five days in the week, or curds made from the whey of milk, which I find is not properly made in the South of England: this curd is obtained by old churn milk (butter milk) poured into whey, scalding hot, the acid of which, uniting the serum, produces a fine, mellow, bland, substance, very wholesome, cooling and nutritive: upon this diet, and upon bread and

milk, the labouring poor in the North of England principally exist."

Elsewhere the author notes farming conditions in the north of the county:

"..the calcareous part of the Moorlands or that on limestone bottom, is pretty extensive, reaching in length from the Weaver Hills to Longnor, and in breadth from Dove to Morredge, including fifteen or sixteen parishes and fifty or sixty square miles. The quantity of limestone here is inexhaustible, being in many places in strata of immense thickness. This is the best part of the Moorlands and the soil seems to have a natural aptitude for producing a fine herbage of grass, and, to the credit of the people here, I must observe, that their breed of cows, of the long horned kind, are generally superior to those in the South of the County."

In the late 17th Century dairy farming in the Derbyshire – Staffordshire region was only one branch of an essentially mixed agrarian economy. An analysis of the probate inventories of 70 farmers in the region showed 42 inventories of persons with cheese presses, tubs, vats, boards, shelves and butter churns. Cheese chambers for storing the produce are specifically mentioned in eight instances, one at Stramshall near Uttoxeter, being described as 'over the porch'.

Expansion of dairying

The expansion of dairying can perhaps be viewed as a movement towards that branch of farming for which the land in the region was most suited, and as a reflection of the growing demand for cheese and butter from the rapidly increasing population of the late 18th Century.

In the Derbyshire Archaeological Journal volume LXXXIX, 1969, Adrian Henstock makes reference to cheese manufacture and manufacture in Derbyshire and North Staffordshire at around this time.

"In South and West Derbyshire and parts of North West Staffordshire, the peasant economy had an almost entirely agricultural basis. Here were a large number of farmers occupying small or medium-sized holdings who were engaged in mixed farming, but with an emphasis on dairying that gradually increased over the period under review."

The importance of dairying in this region was that cheese and butter were produced as items of commerce. In a report for the Board of Agriculture in 1794, Thomas Brown stated explicitly that cheese was *"the chief, if not only, article of provision which natives can spare out of their own county".* Many farmers relied on the proceeds from their dairies to pay their rent.

Cheese made in Derbyshire from around 1794 onwards was 2½in to 3in thick, 14in diameter and weighed 30lb. The staple diet of Peakland miners, it was described as generally mild and in taste, though not always in colour, greatly resembling that made in Gloucestershire. It was also similar to Cheshire and was sold in London masquerading as Cheshire.

Recipe for Derby Cheese 1794

Fresh milk to deep wooden, brass or copper tub about 3ft in main.

Rennet was added to separate curds and whey (this was an acid substance made by the butcher from stomach skins of young calves which had been cleaned, dried and salted).

Curd was broken up by going through a hand-operated cheese mill, salted and put in hoops and subjected to great pressure for some days. In Staffordshire the presses were usually massive square blocks of limestone or gritstone supported by a wooden frame. During the 19th Century this was replaced by a metal lever press.

John Byng, later Viscount Torrington, noted in his diary in 1790 "the cheese of this country pleases me much; being a medium between Cheshire and Stilton". This is the Staffordshire cheese recipe type.

Before the closing years of the 19th Century dairy farming in the region could be virtually equated with cheese and butter manufacture as opposed to liquid milk production, it being impossible to market fresh milk outside the immediate vicinity of the farm because of the inadequacy of transport facilities.

Another view of local agriculture in the 19th Century and the importance of cheesemaking comes in' Past and Present, Staffordshire and Warwickshire', by John Alfred Longford

Staffordshire is not one of the great grain-producing counties; but dairy farming is common. In an interesting article in the Journal of the Royal Agricultural Society, from which nearly all of the following particulars are derived, Mr. H. Evershed says –

"*Excluding the light-hand tract which surrounds the county town (Stafford), and extends from Trentham through Cannock Chase and Lichfield to Tamworth, the county consists chiefly of the cheese-making districts, where pasturage prevails*".

The reason of this is simple. The soil and climate of Staffordshire being much more suitable to the production of grass than of wheat or other corn, dairy farming is more profitable than arable cultivation, which is at once costly and hazardous.

"*During the winter months – from November till the early part of May – milking cows are tied up in the sheds, whereby half the litter required in open yards is saved. The calving time is usually early April, the period most desirable on cheese farms, because the cows are then in full profit at the best time of the year, when the best cheese is made, and when the natural supply of food is greatest (during the summer no artificial food is given, except in bad seasons). Cheese-making is sometimes continued throughout the year, especially in large dairies, but generally the winter's milk is devoted to suckling or butter-making. A first rate cow will yield during the year £14 worth of cheese (at 60s the cost of 120lbs), which, with £2 for the whey butter, £1.10s for whey for pigs and £1 for the calf, makes the total for the produce £18.10s."*

Importance to the economy

In 1829 cheesemaking was described as "the most important article in the economy of Derbyshire and Staffordshire Moorland farms". However farmhouse cheesemaking still remained extremely hard work and was always performed by female labour. Hours were long, often from 5am to 7pm, seven days a week.

Many farmhouses had the equipment for cheesemaking in the kitchen; it took up considerable space, but was convenient for the farmer's wife, when cheese was the main daily product, and helped to keep the cheese warm.

Mrs. Doris Stevenson recalled her grandparents home at Sapperton Manor (1881): *"The kitchen had three huge presses and a huge water pump with a huge brough five feet long; the cheese was stored in a loft and turned every day".*

The Wilde's made cheese at Moss Carr Farm. The cheese was made in the kitchen and stored in the bedrooms and on the stairs.

Improved methods of cheesemaking were evolved by inventive farmers such as George Sheldon of Youlgreave.

Marketing

The marketing of cheese at this time was primarily centred on weekly markets at Derby, Ashbourne, Bakewell, Chesterfield, Uttoxeter, Leek, Burton on Trent, Nottingham or Mansfield. Cheese was sold direct to consumers or local cheesemongers and provision dealers or to the cheese factors. Considerable amounts of cheese also went to London by land or water.

These links with London dated back centuries. The earliest reference, 1686, to the activities of London cheesemongers in the region comes from Dr. Robert Plot describing the North Staffordshire Moorlands remarked "Limestone hills and rich pastures and meadows the great dairies are maintained in this part of Staffordshire that supply Uttoxeter market with such vast quantities of good butter and cheese that the cheesemongers of London have thought it worth their while to set up a factorage here."

As far back as the 17th Century London cheesemongers were spending up to £500 on Derbyshire and Staffordshire cheeses and butter at Uttoxeter market in a single day.

Contemporary commercial directories indicate that in the 19th Century cheese factors were concentrated in Ashbourne, Derby, Uttoxeter and Burton on Trent. In Staffordshire 1851 there were five cheese factors in Burton, Uttoxeter and Longnor.

From farmhouse to factory

The mid 19th Century brought a significant change. Up until then, all cheesemaking was a farmhouse activity, but in 1871 the first UK cheese factory was started by William Gilman at Longford, near Derby.

As Janet Arthur notes in her book 'Say Cheese!': "News of co-operative cheese-making came from America to London in 1868. The English gentry and landowners took up the idea, on behalf of their own tenants and local farmers and the first cheese factories in England began work in Derbyshire."

The new factory at Longford was ideally proportioned at 30ft wide and 60ft long. Liquid animal rennet was used in the Derby cheesemaking factory, whereas at Longford 'skins of rennet' were being bought in 1872.

Mr. Murray, at the Derby factory, recommended that the coagulum cutting knife blades should be no more than quarter-inch apart.

"For the first two or three days after the cheese has been removed from the hoops (moulds or chissetts) it should be daily rubbed over with melted butter in a hot state. If this is neglected, sudden changes in temperature cause the rind of the cheese rapidly to contract, leaving it full of unsightly cracks and fissures, forming a birthplace for flies and a whole host of insect enemies," said Mr Murray.

Farmhouse Derby had a considerable amount of cream removed. This cheese was made at Longford. At Derby they made a full cream American style cheese. In Longford a water wheel was used to turn agitators which kept the milk in constant motion and thus preventing the separation of the cream.

The change from farmhouse to more centralised production is also recounted by Helen Harris in Industrial Archaeology of The Peak District 1904 , which notes just how hard cheesemaking on the farm was. that "during the season cheesemaking was a seven day a week job and involved long hours for the factory managers who were often assisted by their wives".

"The making of butter and cheese for home consumption was carried out for many years on farmhouses of the Peak District. Some of these, particularly on the Derbyshire-Staffordshire border, still retain old cheese presses and other equipment used for manufacture. As the 19th Century progressed and milk became more plentiful, in the absence of satisfactory transport, it could only be suitably marketed by producing long-keeping quality cheese. Prices paid in towns for cheese, however, were often hopelessly low.

The cheese factory at Longford, Derbyshire, which opened on May 4th 1870.

At 30ft by 60ft, the Longford factory was ideally proportioned for cheesemaking.

Cheese and buttermaking and prize cheeses at the dairy show, as shown in the Illustrated London News in 1878.

A means of milk disposal was provided by a number of small cheese factories set up towards the end of the 19th Century. England's first purpose built factory was at Longford near Derby in 1870. Running expenses came from a levy on farm milk supplied to the factory. Derby and Stilton cheeses were the main cheeses made in Derbyshire. The Nuttall and Brindley families ran these cheese factories until 1962. in 1870 the Staffordshire Reapsmoor cheese factory was set up on land given by Mr William Shirley. Wensleydale cheeses were made at Glutton Bridge factory, near Earl Sterndale.

At the turn of the 19th Century cheesemaking took a definite second place to liquid milk as the price of this commodity increased and rail and better road transport were realised".

Cheesemaking factories in Staffordshire late 19th Century

Reapsmoor	Rocester
Ecton	Croxden
Alstonefield	Uttoxeter
Waterhouses	Church Leigh
Mayfield	Hamstall Ridware
Ellastone	

Cheesemaking factories on the Staffordshire/Derbyshire border

Glutton Bridge	Longford
Hartington	Marston Montgomery
Parwich	Sudbury
Grangemill	Sutton on the Hill
Fenny Bentley	Etwall
Windley	Eggington
Ashbourne	Willington
Brailsford	Derby
Kedleston	

Alstonefield and Hopedale

The village of Alstonefield was typical of how cheese making figuresd large in the life on the Staffordshire/Derbyshire border during the 19th Century. Samuel Mellor of Alstonefield, owner of the George Inn when he was declared bankrupt in 1826, was also described as a cheese factor, dealer and chapman, still living in Alstonefield in 1834.

Other Alstonefield cheese factors were Bartholomew Massey in the early 1850s, and Anthony Massey by 1860. A cheese factory was opened at Hopedale in 1878 by 20 local farmers trading as Alstonefield Dairy Association. By 1916 the cheese factory was run by Dovedale Dairy Association Ltd. And by 1924 by Derbyshire Farmers Ltd. It closed in 1930 and was later converted into a private house.

We learn more of cheese making in and around Alstonefield in 'Alstonefield – A Village History' (Alstonefield Local History Society).

This book tells us that the old cheese factory at Hopedale was registered and opened in 1874 by 20 farmers (anyone owning cows was classed as a farmer) and was a move towards co-operative farming. It was originally called The Alstonefield Dairy Association. Later the name was changed to the Dovedale Dairy Association and finally to Derbyshire Farmers. The cheese made was a Derby Cheese which was firm, but had a creamy texture.

In the Staffordshire Directory for 1892, Richard Riley was listed as the manager. The whey settled in vats and was put into a tank, which still exists, at the south west corner of the factory. On top was a bucket pump where people came to collect whey to feed their pigs. The cheese was made in the room at the north end and the stone rennet shelves still exist in the kitchen. The second downstairs room contained racks where the cheeses were turned whilst maturing.

Other factories opened at Glutton Bridge, Ecton, Gratton, Woodeaves, Grangemill and Hartington.

Reapsmoor

In 1840 there was a cheese factory in the township of Reapsmoor, near Sheen, and another in 1844 and 1851.

In 1881 William Shirley had a cheese factory at his farm at Rewlach, and his son Samuel was the first secretary of the Manifold Valley Dairies Association Ltd., which in 1912 had a cheese factory on the Warslow-Longnor. The factory closed in 1958. Making Cheddars, Cheshires, Caerphilly and Derby Cheese, it stayed open well into the 20th Century, operating under the Express Dairies name between 1936 and 1950.

The Reapsmoor factory, was run on co-operative lines. A number of farmers contributed labour towards its construction, others bought £5 shares. However as with any cheese factory, the success or failure of the enterprise rested on the skill of the cheesemaker. Mrs Gilman started the cheesemaking at Reapsmoor, the Gilman family being associated with local cheesemaking for 50 years.

William Sutton and his son John made cheese at Reapsmoor from 1880 to 1884

Cheesemakers at work inside the factory at Reapsmoor, opened in the mid 19th Century.

Giant Cheddars in Green's cheese shop in St Edward Street, Leek.

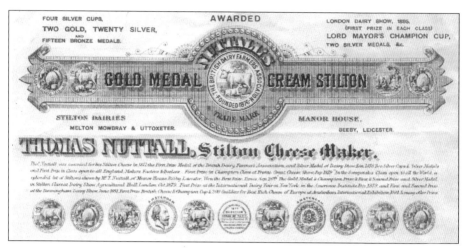

An 1880's billhead of Thomas Nuttall from Beeby, Leicestershire, who was also making 'Stilton" at Uttoxeter.

while their brother-in-law Colin Lownds managed the Glutton Bridge factory, making Wensleydale cheese.

Hartington

John Marriott Nuttall reopened the Hartington factory to make Stilton cheese in 1900.

In 1911 there was a serious problem of discolouration in cheese, this was eventually traced to the lack of an efficient water supply. The ponds which gave the water were normally situated immediately below the farm manure heap. This caused contaminated cheese equipment and milk.

Four years later, the cleanliness of dairies was addressed in the 1915 Milk and Dairies Act which depended on recent developments of microbiology to detect infected, contaminated or dirty milk.

The cheeses made in the Staffordshire Moorlands were: Staffordshire (mainly on farms), Cheshire, Cheddar, American factory-made Cheddar, factory made Derbyshire, farmhouse Derbyshire (which had half the fat removed from the milk), Caerphilly, Stilton at Hartington and a Uttoxeter Stilton made by Mr Dainton. The Cheddar made by the American method had cheese leaving the factory in eight weeks or less.

Forty two inventories of cheesemaking equipment were found across the Staffordshire Moorlands and borders with Derbyshire.

Rocester, Brailsford and others

Thomas Nuttall made Stilton cheese at the Manor Farm, Beeby and also at Uttoxeter in Staffordshire. Currently there are four cheesemakers in Staffordshire and only one in Derbyshire (Hartington).

John Dainton was manager of Great Western and Metropolitan dairies in Uttoxeter where Derby, Stilton and a Staffordshire cheese were made.

About fifty farmers set up Egginton Factory in Derbyshire.

Mrs Keeling came to Rocester in 1920 as cheesemaker, later becoming manager. She was trained in Somerset. In 1920 cheeses from Rocester went to Soho in London. They weighed up to a hundredweight. The cheesemaker and manager, Mrs Keeling made mostly Cheshire – one hundredweight and smaller 30lb Derbyshires.

There were three big vats which held 500 gallons. Sometimes she had to fill them twice daily when milk volumes were high. Fole Dairy, near Uttoxeter, was also in operation at this time.

At Sutton on the Hill in 1912, Mr William Twigg helped Mr George Sharp to make cheese and also drove one of the wagons. There were two other wagon drivers. They used to have a pair of horses for fetching different rounds or sometimes a load of cheese. William Twigg used to measure the milk into churns, lock it up and take it to the train station at Etwall for Cadbury's. April and May time there used to be a big flush of milk and it came to Sutton on the Hill to be made into cheese.

Up to 1913 a lot of farmers sold the milk to Nestlé at Tutbury and the milk not sold was run to Mickleover station by horse and cart. There were two farmers in the village who supplied drays to take the milk to Tutbury, down through Sutton.

Sometimes, when they were coming back through Hatton, the men used to stop and used to have to pull the lids of the churns to see whether they were coming or going, they used to get that much beer, four pence a quart. In 1913 the price that Nestle offered was so bad that the farmers got together and started Brailsford Dairy Farmers Association to make cheese and sell milk. In 1917, through the co-operative movement, they obtained a contract to sell 680 gallons a day to the co-operative in Birmingham. They bought a new Leyland lorry for £1,000 and saved a £1,000 a year versus rail delivery. They bought a second lorry!

At Brailsford, a rather tall, 82lb cheese was made called Cheddar. They also made a flat 40lb Derbyshire, 20 inches across and 18 inches high. The Cheddar was given light pressing on day 1, day 2 increased pressure, day 3 increased pressure again.

The cheese factory at Brailsford was very successful and an employee remembers receiving a £14 bonus in 1937. At Brailsford they made a Derby cheese which won the London Dairy Show on numerous occasions.

Mr Rodgers reported: "We used to go up to Brailsford North, Mercaston and Hulland which was on sand and gravel and there was more herbage in the grass. I mean burnet, chips parsley, chicory, yarrow. They were the herbs to guarantee good quality milk, its not the cream. It's the solids, not the fats, and herbage will make solids not fats."

The cheese was not fit for sale for four to five months. The cheese was turned every day for two weeks, then every two days for four weeks and then three days and so on. If you neglect turning the cheese the acidity settles on the bottom and causes a red tint. At grading the cheeses were always on the floor and the buyers used to walk on them! You could tell the quality of the cheese by treading on it.

In 1915 Wilts United Dairies of Trowbridge became involved with many local dairies. Leonard Maggs controlled and managed the company.

The system rationalised

For the farmer finding a milk buyer was an annual anxiety. For the farmer's wife cheesemaking was still a burden.

In 1934 the Milk Marketing Board was formed and farmers were assured of a regular income and a definite outlet for their milk. Surplus milk was moved around the country to processing factories. Where it was condensed, evaporated or turned into cheese. The whole system was rationalised on a national basis.

By 1945 small scale cheesemaking had declined due to two main reasons:

1. Milk Marketing Boards were ensuring a guaranteed milk price to the farmer.

2. Railways – you could get a better price for liquid milk if you sent it to London.

I believe that now the Milk Marketing Boards have disappeared milk producers face fierce milk pricing policies and really it is time to make cheese again or some other on-farm product if reasonable returns and standards of living are to be achieved for the future.

Chapter Three

The Principles of Cheesemaking

 **A step-by-step guide to cheese types, the cheesemaking process, setting up a plant, cheese recipes and the key stages in making cheese.**

Following the long history of cheesemaking on Staffordshire farms and in small factories (14) there are now only four cheesemakers in Staffordshire.

Innes Cheese, Highfields Farm Dairy, Clifton Lane, Statfold, nr Tamworth, Staffordshire B79 0AQ

Stella Bennett and her son make cheese daily using only the fresh drawn milk from their herd of 300 goats.

They are perhaps best known for their individual lemony fresh Innes Button – twice Supreme Champion in the British Cheese Awards. They also make the Gold Medal winning Bosworth Leaf and the smaller Clifton Leaf, which are richly flavoured and mould ripened. Their final cheese is the milder nutty Bosworth Ash matured with a sprig of rosemary.

Stella explained: *"Our cheese make is based on French recipes where the warm goat's milk comes straight from the milking parlour to our cheesemaking facility. We believe that using the fresh goat's milk has a considerable effect on our cheese quality and taste."*

Staffordshire Organic Cheese, Newhouse Farm, Acton, Newcastle-under-Lyme, Staffordshire ST5 4EE

David Deaville makes a raw milk organic cheddar type cheese using British cows' milk and a specialist ewes' milk cheese.

Franjoy Cheese Dairy, nr Stone, Staffordshire

The Wagner family make a range of flavoured cheese using milk from their own Jersey dairy herd. The cheese flavours include: chives, cracked black pepper, apricot, garlic and herb, smoked garlic, ginger, walnut and pineapple. The basic cheese is a Cheddar type.

The Staffordshire Cheese Company Limited, Churnet View Business Park, Cheddleton, nr. Leek, Staffordshire

John Knox started this company in 1989 to re-introduce cheesemaking to the Staffordshire Moorlands.   In 2002 he launched the Staffordshire cheese at the Staffordshire Show. This was to a recipe originally used from the 18th Century. John and his son Simon developed ten cheeses, including: Archie's Choice (crumbly), Oaked Smoked cheese, blue cheese, cheese with additives including chives and beer and goats cheese. Archie's Choice won first prize in its class at the Bakewell Show and the other cheeses have won medals at the British Cheese Awards. The company was sold to Adrian Corke and Sue Carline, local brewers, in 2004.

Cheese types

The cheese recipes, which are included in this chapter, relate to cheeses made in Staffordshire in past centuries and the cheeses made by The Staffordshire Cheese Company at the present time.

Staffordshire Cheese

Re-introduced in May 2002 by John Knox. Launched at Staffordshire Show in that year.

Characteristics

Hard pressed, soft, creamy, open-textured cheese being a cross between a white Stilton and a Wensleydale.

Milk Treatment

The cheese is made from Staffordshire cows' milk with a little cream added, before mixing and pasteurising at 72 – 75°C for 15 seconds.

Starter

0.2 to 0.4% mixed culture added to milk at 32°C ± 1°C.

Ripen

1 hour to 1 hour 15 minutes.

Rennet

32°C ± 1°C. Quantity 20mls single strength (Chy Max)/100 litres of milk. Dilute 6 to 8 times with clean water.

Cutting

Curd firmness is checked with a sharp knife by cutting and lifting the coagulum. A clean solid coagulum break means ready for cutting. This takes 35 to 45 minutes. Cut with horizontal knife in same manner. Curd particles size of large beans. Cutting time 8-10 minutes.

Stirring/Scald

Stir curds at 30 – 32°C for 40 minutes.

Pitching/drawing whey

Settle curds and start drawing whey through sieve at end of vat. Time: 35 minutes. At completion of whey off acidity 0.29% lactic acid.

Texturing

Break the curds every 15 minutes over a period of 45 minutes. Acidity at first break 0.39%, second break 0.45%, final break 0.53% lactic acid.

Milling

Curd broken using stainless steel pegmill.

Salting

2.5% salt added to curds during milling. Salt mixed by turning curds using a food grade plastic shovel on one occasion and turning by hand on three occasions. No more than this to avoid drying out the curds.

Moulding

Salted cheese curds are hand filled to muslin cloth lined stainless steel moulds. The cloths have been sewn into a tube before lining the mould and inserting a circular cloth base. The moulds were specially made by Staffordshire tradesmen to achieve correct cheese shape and whey drainage.

Pressing

The cheeses are pressed at 2lbs/sq inch and temperature of 21 – 25'C overnight.

Storage

After pressing, the cheese cloth is smoothly covering the cheese surface. The cheeses are then covered in a vegetarian fat to prevent cracking and rapid drying out. The cheeses are stored at 9 – 10°C, turned daily for one week and weekly thereafter. The mild cheese is ripe in 2 to 4 weeks and can be matured up to 12 months.

Characteristics

Fine surface rind, slightly open texture and lemony flavour in young cheese, changing to dense full flavour in mature variety.

Analysis

Fat 31.5% average

Moisture 41.5% average

Dry matter 58.5% average

Fat in dry matter 53.8% average

Tolerance ±4%

Classification of cheeses (ref. Dairy handbook Alfa-Laval 1990)

It is difficult to classify all the various existing types of cheese, as there are many borderline cases. The following criteria are normally used:

- **Method of coagulating casein in curd-making**; we distinguish between rennet and acid cheese. Some types of cheese are produced with both lactic acid and rennet. They are called acid rennet cheeses. Cottage cheese belongs to this category.

- **Moisture content**; we distinguish between hard, semi-hard and soft cheese. The moisture content is low in hard cheeses such as Parmesan, Cheddar and Emmental. It is much higher in soft cheeses such as Camembert and Brie.

- **Principal micro-organisms used for ripening**; most cheese types are ripened by means of lactic acid bacteria. There are, however, cheese types which are also ripened by means of other micro-organisms. Tilsit, Port Salut and St. Paulin for example, are finally ripened by micro-organisms smeared on the surfaces, blue veined cheeses such as Roquefort and Gorgonzola by blue moulds and Camembert by white moulds.

- **Texture of the cheese**; we distinguish between round-eyed, granular and close-textured cheese. The holes or eyes in cheese are formed by certain lactic-acid bacteria which, during the ripening process, develop carbon dioxide as a fermentation by-product. The carbon dioxide collects in interstices in the curd. Air will be entrapped between the curd grains if the curd is moulded into cheese in the atmosphere. Carbon dioxide will then collect in these interstices and form 'granular' eyes. Tilsit is an example of a granular cheese.

If the cheese is moulded below the surface of the whey, in order to exclude air, the interstices will be fewer in number, and the carbon dioxide forms round holes, eyes, when the curd is pressed. Gouda is an example of a round eyed cheese.

A close-textured hard cheese is made with starter cultures which emit very little or no carbon dioxide. All the lactose is then fermented before the final forming takes place. The most well known type of close-textured hard cheese is Cheddar cheese. Holes can be found in mature Cheddar cheese, but they have a mechanical origin, caused by the processing technique.

Setting up your cheese plant

Cheesemaking courses are run on a regular basis by Chris Ashby at Reaseheath College, near Nantwich. If you are serious about starting a cheese enterprise, it is recommended that you attend one of these cheese courses at an early stage in your planning.

At the Staffordshire Cheese Company we brought milk in from local farms and converted it into cheese. If you are going to make cheese on the farm from your own milk it is recommended that milking cows is one activity and making cheese is another, it is not possible for one person to carry out both activities.

It is essential to involve the Environmental Health Officer at the earliest stages of setting up your cheese manufacturing. It is also strongly recommended that you use an appropriately qualified and experienced cheese technology consultant. This can save many headaches and lost time in progressing planning permission, monitoring building set up and costs and also preparing a robust HACCP with the Environmental Health Officers and cheesemaker.

Some farmers have reported 12 month delays from start of building to having an EU number and saleable cheese. Normally planning of the cheese room, types of cheeses to make, capital and revenue costs, links with Environmental Health Officers, Trading Standards Officers (for cheese label information) and builders takes place over a six month period. When our cheese room was set up, the EU number was awarded in the same time span and all cheeses made were saleable from the start, e.g. soft cheeses in a few weeks, hard cheeses in 2 to 12 months depending on maturing period of the cheese.

The process of cheesemaking is an ancient craft that dates back thousands of years. Cheesemaking combines both 'art' and science'.

The cheesemaking process

All cheeses are made using the same basic technology of:

- Good quality raw milk
- Pasteurising the milk
- Acidifying the milk through the addition of lactic acid producing bacteria (starter cultures)
- Adding a coagulant (historically animal rennet but nowadays mostly microbial rennet) to form curds and whey
- Cutting, stirring or heating the curds to release more whey as required
- Draining the whey
- Pouring the curds into moulds which may involve 'cheddaring', milling and

salting the curds first
- In the case of hard cheeses, pressing the formed cheeses to remove more whey
- Wrapping the finished cheese in plastic, bandage, wax or some other material; or in the case of white mould or washed rind cheeses treating the coats to accelerate the ripening of the cheese or to help form a crust or coat on the cheese
- Maturing the cheese for the required period depending on the cheese

The manufacture of artisan cheeses

The process of cheesemaking is an ancient craft that dates back thousands of years. Cheesemaking combines both 'art' and 'science'.

The basic stages of cheesemaking

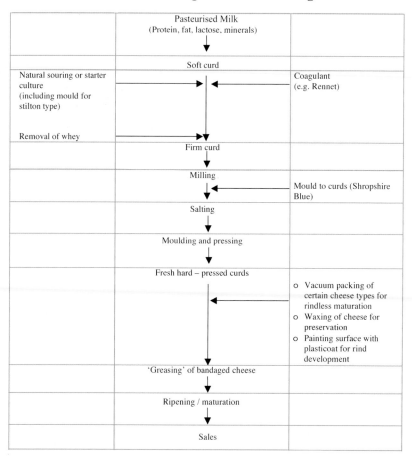

	Pasteurised Milk (Protein, fat, lactose, minerals) ↓	
	Soft curd	
Natural souring or starter culture (including mould for stilton type)	→← ↓	Coagulant (e.g. Rennet)
Removal of whey	→ ↓↓	
	Firm curd ↓	
	Milling ↓←	Mould to curds (Shropshire Blue)
	Salting ↓	
	Moulding and pressing ↓	
	Fresh hard – pressed curds ← ↓	o Vacuum packing of certain cheese types for rindless maturation o Waxing of cheese for preservation o Painting surface with plasticoat for rind development
	'Greasing' of bandaged cheese ↓	
	Ripening / maturation ↓	
	Sales	

(Full fat hard cheese)

Cheese manufacturing table (ref. Dairy Microbiology – National Dairy Council 1981)

The undernoted figures are not rigidly adhered to by every cheesemaker and therefore should be used as a guide. Factors such as seasonal variations, regional conditions and starter culture activity influence the cheesemaking controls. Experience

CHEESE	MILK TEMP. WHEN STARTER IS ADDED	QUANTITY OF STARTER ADDED	RIPENING PERIOD	AT TIME OF RENNETING		QUANTITY OF RENNET ADDED (MLS PER 1000 LTRS OF MILK	TIME REQUIRED TO REACH DESIRED COAGULUM	SCALD TEMP.	MAKE TIME (RENNET TO SALT TIME)	ACIDITY AT SALTING (% LACTIC ACID)	MATURING TIME (APPROX)
				ACIDITY (1% LACTIC ACID)	TEMP.						
Caerphilly	31°C	1.0%	¾ - 1hr	0.20 – 0.22	31°C	200-250	40 mins	32°C - 34°C	2¼ - 2¾ hrs	0/51 – 0.55	2 weeks
Cheddar	30°C	1.0 - 1.5%	½ - 1hr	0.19 – 0.21	30°C	220-250	45 mins	38°C - 42°C	3¾ - 4¼ hrs	0.60 – 0.70	3-5 months (mild) 5 months or more (mature)
Cheshire	30°C	1.5 - 2.0%	1 – 1½ hrs	0.19 – 0.21	30°C	180	30 mins	32°C – 34°C	3 – 3 ½ hrs	0.60 – 0.70	1 – 3 months
Derby	29°C	1.5%	¼ - ½ hr	0.20	29°C	300	45 mins	36°C – 38°C	3¾ - 4¼ hrs	0.65 – 0.70	3 – 4 months
Double Gloucester	30°C	1.0 - 2.0%	1 hr	0.18 – 0.19	30°C	220-300	40 mins	37°C - 38°C	3¾ - 4¼ hrs	0.58 – 0.65	3 – 6 months
Lancashire	30°C	2.0 – 2.5%	½ - 1 hr	0.185 - 0.220	30°C	220 - 250	50 mins	34°C - 38°C	3¼ - 3¾ hrs	0.80 – 0.85	4 – 8 weeks or more
Leicester	30°C	1.0 – 1.5%	1 hr	0.20	30°C	300	45 mins	36°C - 38°C	3¾ - 4¼ hrs	0.55 – 0.60	10 – 12 weeks
Stilton	30°C	0.01%	½ - 1 hr	Must not exceed 0.17	30°C	200	1 – 1½ hrs	Not scalded	Overnight (22 – 24 hrs)	1.10 – 1.30	3 weeks (white) 3 – 6 months (blue)
Wensleydale	30°C	1.5%	1 – 1½ hrs	0.19	30°C	120 – 180	45 mins	32°C - 34°C	2¾ - 3¼ hrs	0.52 – 0.62	3 weeks (white) 6 months (blue)

of the cheesemaker and evaluation of the final matured cheese will enable decisions to be taken on ideal temperatures, times and acidity levels. Suppliers of starter cultures, such as Chr Hansen, Rhodia Texel, Cargil-Texturising Solutions, are also a valuable source of cheesemaking and recipe development.

Milk as basic material

Milks from different species of mammals have been used for the manufacture of cheese and Table 1 illustrates the major differences in the chemical composition of these milks. As a result, variations in the quality of the cheese do occur, depending on the type of milk used. For example, milk containing high total solids (sheep) increases cheese yield, and conversely, milk high in fat produces softer cheese, but improves the mouth-feel of the product. Thus the cheesemaking process has to be modified in relation to the type of milk used.

Table 1

Chemical composition (%) of milks of selected species of mammals

Animal	Fat	Protein	Milk Sugar	Minerals
Cow	3.8	3.0	4.8	0.75
Goat	6.0	3.3	4.6	0.84
Sheep	9.0	4.6	4.7	1.00
Buffalo	6.0	3.8	4.5	0.75

Data compiled by Scott (1986)

Milk for cheesemaking is carefully selected to make sure that there are no antibiotics or harmful agents that could affect the process. Raw milk cheese may be made or the milk heated and held at 65°C for 30 minutes (batch pasteurisation) or 72°C minimum for 15 seconds (high temperature short time pasteurisation). The purpose of pasteurisation is to destroy any harmful bacteria.

Special starter cultures are then added to warmed milk (around 30°C) and these change some of the milk sugar into lactic acid. The culture acidifies the milk at a fast rate and prepares it for renneting (mainly chymosin). When the rennet is added it produces a coagulum, similar to a thick jelly, in about 40 minutes.

When the coagulum is sufficiently set it is cut into pieces using special knives. This action releases much of the liquid whey held in the curd. The textural quality of the finished cheese is determined partially by the size of the pieces of curd produced during the cutting process. The cut pieces are heated to start a curd shrinking process, which with the steady production of lactic acid from the starter cultures, will change it into small rice-sized grains for Cheddar or Caerphilly and the bean sized pieces for, say, Cheshire and Wensleydale with Lancashire and Leicestershire between these sizes.

At a carefully chosen point the curd particles are allowed to fall to the bottom of the cheese vat, the left over liquid, which consists of water, milk, sugar and albumen (now called whey) is drained off and the curd allowed to mat together to form slabs of curd.

The slabs are either milled (Cheddar) at a specific acidity, or broken by hand at 15 minute intervals to an acidity of around 0.45% lactic acid (Staffordshire,Wensleydale, Derby, Leicester) before milling and salting to provide flavour and help preserve the cheese.

The salted curds are filled to a suitable size and shape of mould and pressed at appropriate pressure. Hard cheeses are held at a specified temperature (10°C) for maturing and for blue cheeses at 10 – 14°C and humidity of 85 to 95%.

Cheddar cheesemaking (Method used in the West of Scotland)

Characteristics
Hard pressed close-textured cheese with a firm body and strong full flavour. May be coloured or white.

Milk treatment
The milk should be freshly pasteurised and ripened at 30 - 31°C (86 – 88°F) according to season and weather. Any milk over .20% l.a. should be rejected for cheesemaking.

Manufacturing details

Starter: 1 – 2%	Rennet: 4oz/100 gallons	Annatto: 4oz/100 gallons
STAGE	% ACIDITY	TIMES
Raw milk	0.15 – 0.20	Adding starter to renneting
At renneting	Increase of 0.02 – 0.25	20 mins. – 1¼ hours
At cutting	0.12 – 0.14	Renneting to cutting
		35 – 50 mins.
At scald	Increase of 0.015 – 0.02	Cutting to scald 1 – 1¼ hours
At settling	0.18 – 0.19	Scalding to pitching
		15 – 40 mins.
At running	0.21 – 0.23 S.S.)	Pitching to running
	0.25 – 0.26 M.S.)	15 – 30 mins.
At milling	0.70 – 0.75	Running to milling
		1¾ – 2 hours

Cutting the curd
The curd particle size should be small and uniform without slashing it to produce unnecessary small particles which would be lost in the whey.

Scalding

The heating should commence 10 to 15 mins. After cutting, raising the temperature gradually to 39 – 40°C (103 to 104°F) in 1 to 1¼ hours from starting cutting.

Running

The whey is drawn at an acidity of 0.21 – 0.23 in 2¾ to 3 hours from renneting
- single-strain starter 0.26-0.30 in 2¾ to 3 hours
- mixed and multi-strain starter

Cheddaring

The matted curd should be channelled down the centre of the vat to promote rapid and even drainage of the whey, cut into uniform sized blocks in 20-30 minutes, and the blocks interchanged in position every 10 to 15 minutes until an acidity of 0.70 to 0.75 is reached for milling. The curd should be well mellowed, close textured and give a hot iron draw with threads 1½ to 1¾ in length. It should be foliated and torn apart into long strips the entire block length, similar to the breast of chicken.

Milling, salting and hooping

The curd should be milled rapidly to avoid any further increase in acidity and stirred for up to 10 minutes to allow the fat to solidify and to avoid off-flavours in the curd; salt added at the rate of 2 to 2¼lbs/100 gallons milk, thoroughly stirred into the mass of shipped curd and packed into the moulds at 75 to 80°F.

Curing

3 to 6 months, depending on storage conditions, acidity, whilst good quality cheese will improve with up to 2 years storage.

Cheshire (method used at Aston, Cheshire)

I.   The temperature of pasteurisation of the cheese milk is 72°C (161°F) for 15 seconds (minimum).

II.   Temperature of milk when it is run into the vat is 31°C (88°F).

III.   The starter used must have been inoculated and kept at between 20 – 33.5°C (68 – 92°F), the optimum temperature for culture growth. The acidity of the powder starter must be between 0.9° and 1.20°. The smell must be clean and acidic with no putrefactive odours. The appearance should be of a thick granular paste with no 'wheying off'. Although these tests give the cheesemaker some idea of the nature of the starter he is going to use, the only really absolute tests of the starter's condition are those employed by the laboratory and these would be so long in bringing results as to make the idea invalid.

IV.   After the starter is added, the vat of milk plus starter are allowed to ripen for 1 to 1½ hours. This is necessary to allow the bacteria to proceed with their reactions.

V.   The acidity at renneting is approximately 0.18. Rennet, diluted with 10 times its volume of water is added. The rennet is stirred into the milk for 4 – 5 minutes only and then agitation stopped.

VI.   The length of time allowed for coagulation is 35 minutes.

VII.   The coagulum is cut for 8 minutes before the steam is put on.

VIII.   The scald temperature is 32.5 – 33.5°C (91– 92°F). The stirring speed should be as fast as possible without spilling the curds and whey over the sides of the vat.

IX.   At the end of the scald period the vat is pitched, i.e. agitation is stopped. The acidity should be around 0.14.

X.   The curd is left under the whey from anything between 10 and 25 minutes.

XI.   The whey is run off at 33°C (91°F) and the curd acidity should be around 0.21.

XII.   The cheese is broken a) to control the speed at which the bacterial reactions are going and b) to remove the whey from the curd. If this is not done the acidity speeds up and if done too fast the acidity drops, i.e. slows down - takes much longer to reach the optimum acidity.

XIII.   The curd should be milled at acidity 0.68 to 0.72 and its appearance should be slightly moist and when torn gives a leafy appearance.

XIV.   The curd is salted to bring the acid reaction to a very slow rate, it helps to preserve the cheese and adds flavour.

XV.   Cheeses are made in moulds a) for convenience re ease of handling, b) provides a container for the cheese so that the whey can be expelled from the curd more easily. The cheese is pressed to enable the excess whey to be drained out. Cheshire cheeses are stored at 9 to 11°C (48 – 52°F) and at a humidity of 85% RH minimum.

They are allowed to mature for 10 to 14 days under these conditions before they are graded.

Caerphilly (Scott 1982)

Normal cheese are made from 40.9 litres (9 gallons) of milk. Weight 3-4 kg (7-9lb). Flat round shape. 25cm (10in.) diameter x 6cm (2.5in.)

Rind	Thin
Curd	White
Texture Flavour and aroma	Close with open spaces Milk, pleasantly acid
Milk	Mixed, 3.2-3.5% fat. Heat treated to 71.6°C (161°F) for 15 s. Cool to 32.2°C (90°F).
Starter *Ripening* *Rennet*	Amount: 0.25% mixed cultures (in winter 1-1.25%). Variable, 10-90 min. – normally 45 min. at 32.2°C. Temperature, 32.2°C. Rennet, 25-30ml (diluted with 200ml water) per 100 litres (22 gallons) to set in 40-45 mins. Acidity 0.19-0.21%.
Cutting	Cut both ways with vertical knife, 6mm (0.25 in.) blades. Allow whey to rise then cut with horizontal knife. Acidity 0.13-0.14%. Curd firm.
Scald	Scald to 33.3 – 34.4°C (92 – 94°F) in 20-30 min. Stir until dry, i.e. no pocket of whey inside curd, or until imprint of hand remains on pressed curd (approximately 45 – 50 min). Acidity 0.15 – 0.165% (winter 0.18 – 0.185%).
Drawing whey	Acidity 0.2 – 0.21%. Curd scooped to conical mass at corners of vat and also along vat sides.
Texturing	Curd cones cut with long knife and pieces of curd piled along vat sides. Curd broken up or disturbed until acidity is 0.22 – 0.24%.
Milling	Some cheesemakers prefer to cut or break curd, others mill in coarse mill. Acidity 0.28 – 0.40%. Summer to winter.
Salting	1% salt is mixed in the curd (42g (1.5oz) per 4kg (9lb) cheese) (Note that a small quantity of salt is also used to rub onto the cheese while it is being turned in the press.).
Moulding	Mould lined with fine calico with extra steel 'collar'. Curd packed evenly.
Pressing	Light pressure only at first, 12k N/mÇ (2.5cwt per cheese). In 10-12 min. turn and rub cheese with salt. (Note: only half normal salt is used in the curd.) Turn several times with increasing pressure. Finally leave overnight in press at 49.8k N/mÇ (10cwt per cheese).
Brine bath	Cheese removed from mould and cloth and placed in brine bath (strength 18%) at 15.6°C (60°F) for 12 – 24 hours to give 2% salt in the curd.
Storage	The cheese are dried off from the brine bath, and, before sale, rubbed with rye flour/lime mixture to coat and keep dry. Temperature 10-12.6° (50 – 53°F), ripe in 10-14 days.
Characteristics	Mild flavour, fairly close texture. Slightly mouldy coat. 18kg (40lb) in 100 litres water. Add each day sufficient to maintain strength. Discard when the brine becomes cloudy.

Derby (Scott 1982)

Flat, round or block shape cheese 41cm (16in.) diameter x 11.5cm (4.5in.). Almost a quick-ripening Cheddar.

Milk	Farmhouse: good quality mixed raw milk, 136 litres (30 gallons) per cheese. Factory: mixed, pasteurised at 71.6°C (161°F) for 15 seconds, cool to 29°C (84°F).
Starter	Mixed culture of lactic organisms, 1.0 –1.75% added at a temperature of 21°C (70°F).
Ripening	Temperature 29°C for $^3/_4$ – 1 hour according to amount of starter added. Acidity 0.165 – 0.18%, or a rise of 0.01%.
Rennetting	Dilute rennet with 5 – 6 times amount of water. 25 – 30 ml per 100 litres (22 gallons). Temperature 29°C.
Cutting	After 40 – 50 minutes when curd breaks cleanly cut both lengthwise and crosswise 12.5mm (0.5in.) blade. Stir and then cut crosswise. Curd larger and firmer than Cheddar, but more fragile. Acidity 0.12 – 0.13%.
Scald	Stir for 15 min. then scald to 35 – 36°C (95 – 97°F), taking 1 hour. Keep the curd particles free until broken curd shows no free whey pockets inside the cubes.
Running whey	If the curd is firm it may be pitched until the acidity is 0.15 – 0.18% at which time the whey is removed.
Dry stirring	If the curd is still fragile hence stir carefully to allow all free whey to drain off. This is important if 'block' cheeses are being made.
Texturing	Pile curd into half the vat. Cut into four blocks and turn each over. At 10-20 min. intervals turn over and pile the blocks double until the curd shows leafy texture, moist but little free whey.
Milling	Mill once through coarse mill.
Salting	At acidity of 0.45 – 0.55%, salt the curd – 1.8% on dry curd, 2.0% on wet curd. Temperature 25.5°C (78°F). Wet curds lose salt in pressing hence apply more. Allow salt to dissolve before moulding.
Pressing	Moulds 41cm (16in.) diameter x 15cm (6in.) deep with split collar. Press in coarse hessian cloth at 24.9kN/mÇ (5cwt per cheese). Turn in 2h to calico cloth and press at 49.8kN/mÇ (10cwt per cheese) increasing to 74.7kN/mÇ (15cwt per cheese) over-night. Next day turn into tubular bandage and press at 124.5 – 149.4kNmÇ (25 – 30cwt per cheese) for 24h. Iron on a paper cap and convey to store. Alternative is to paste on a calico bandage. Storage temperature 10 – 12.8°C (50 – 55°F). Some cheese may be in block form and a film wrapping is used inside a cardboard container.
Characteristics	Medium acid cheese – not pasty or chalky. Texture close. Full milk flavour at 4 months. Ripe cheese becomes covered with grey green mould on the rind.

Faults	High acid milk or curds produce dry acid crumbly cheese.
	Wet curd at moulding provides soft cheese which dries out to give cracked coats growing mould.
	Poor quality milk (3.1% fat) gives chalky cheese.
	Sweet (low acid) curds favour taint-producing bacteria. Some produce discoloured curds.
	Weed and feed taints are transmitted to the curd.

Abbey Delight (Camembert type) (Chr. Hansen recipe)

Milk	High quality cow's milk is used. The milk is standardised to 2.8% milk fat.	
Heat treatment	Heat treat at 64 – 68°C (147 – 154°F) for 15-20 sec. Cool to 8 – 14°C (46 – 57°F).	
Cold pre-ripening	Add 200-500g/5,000L F-DVS or 100-250u of FD-DVS/5,000L of milk. The cultures to be used are Flora-Danica. Hold for 15-16 hours at 12°C (54°F). After pre-ripening, pH should be around 6.6-6.5.	
Heat treatment	After pre-ripening the milk is pasteurised at 72°C (162°F) for 15 – 20 sec.	
Temperature	Cool to 33-34°C (91 – 93°F) after pasteurisation.	
Additives	3 – 7gm of CaCl2 per 100 litres of milk	
Mould	Penicillium candidum: PCa 1, PCa 3 or PCa FD, 3 – 5u/1,000 litres	
	Geotrichum cadidum: GEO CD 1 or GEO CE 0.5 – 1u/1,000 litres	
Other ripening cultures	Depending on requested flavour, yeast or brevibacterium cultures may be applied.	
	Yeast:	LAF 4, LAF5 or LAF 6 1u/1,000 litre
	Brevibacterium linens:	BL 2 0.25 – 0.5u/1,000 litre
	Brevibacterium casei:	BC 1 – 5u/1,000 litres
Culture	The following cultures and inoculation levels are recommended.	
	Freeze-dried DVS	FLORA-DANICA 750 – 1,000u/5000 litres OR
	Frozen DVS	CH-N 12, CH-N 13, CH-N 14 or FLORA DANICA 750 – 1,000g/5,000 litres
Pre-ripening	Let the milk rest for 45-60 min.	

Rennet	Liquid	NATUREN Standard Plus 140 15 – 25ml per 100 litres of milk or CHY-MAX Plus 125 ml per 100 litre of milk
	Powder	CHY-MAX Powder Extra 1-3g per 100 litres of milk or NATUREN Standard Plus 900 2-6g per 100 litres of milk
	A milk gel forms in 30 – 45mins.	
Cutting	Cut into 20-25 mm cubes when pH reaches 6.0	
Stirring	Allow to stand for 30-50 min with occasional very gentle stirring.	
Whey off	Remove about 30% of the whey.	
Moulding	Ladle the curd from the vat into moulds when pH reaches approx 5.6. First turn after one hour. Second turn after three hours. Third turn after nine hours. The temperature should drop by 1°C (34°F) down to 18-20°C (64-68°F).	
Salting	Remove the curd from the moulds and immerse in brine. Brine: 22°Be, 10°C (50°F), 1-2 hours depending on the size. Dry salting can also be applied.	
Mould	Spray the cheese with PCa 1, PCa 3 or PCa FD 2u/100kg of cheese. (dilute the culture in sterile water with 9g/litre of NaCl – shake – use the same day).	
Storage	Ripen at 14 – 15°C (57-59°F) and 85% RH for one day followed by 8-9 days at 10-13°C (50-55°F) and 95% RH. When a satisfactory mould growth is obtained, dry the cheese surface, pack and store at 4°C (39°F).	
Packaging	Each cheese is packed in grease-proof paper and placed in a cardboard or chip box.	

Hard Goat's Cheese
Made to Staffordshire Cheese recipe. (See page 26)

St Paulin – France (ref. R. Scott "Cheesemaking Practice" 1982)

Derived from Port du Salut cheese made in a Monastery near Laval in France. Semi-hard cheese, flat, round shape, one size 20cm (8in) diameter x 5cm (2in), weight 2kg (4-5lb).

A variety of this type of cheese was produced using Staffordshire milk and sold to local hotels, restaurants and pubs for use in cooking.

Rind: Smooth rind with cloth marks, yellow to orange in colour.

Curd: Creamy white

Flavour/Aroma: Mild flavour, slightly acid with delicate aromatic aroma.

Method:

*   Cow's milk is pasteurised and cooled to 30 – 32°C and 1.5 – 2% mesophilic lactic starter and 1% of an aroma bacterial culture (i.e. Leuconostoc citrovonum) added. 1-2ml/100 litres of annatto may also be added in water.

*   After 1 – 1.25 hours when the acidity has reached 0.22% (pH 6.5), 30 mls of rennet / 100 litres of milk is added. The curd should be firm in 30 minutes.

*   Cut coagulum in 20 minutes to 5mm cubes with wire frame or bladed knife. Stir to float the curd and leave to settle.

*   Take of 50% of the whey, i.e. down to the curd level. Replace the whey with water at 30°C used 0.02% sodium nitrate and sodium chloride in the wash water.

*   Scald the curds by warming to 36 – 39°C for 15 minutes with stirring to firm up the curd to wheat grain size. Settle the curd.

*   Press the curd in the vat using stainless steel plates or food grade plastic sheets for 10 – 15 minutes. then cut pieces of curd to fill moulds.

*   Press the cheese for 2 to 14 hours and increase pressure from 2.5 to 5 cwt per cheese. Cool the cheese while in the press to 28°C, acidity 0.105%.

*   Brine salt (22% salt) the cheese at 10 to 15°C for 15 to 18 hours.

Ripen at 12 – 13°C. Wash the rind for 3 to 4 days with anti-mould solution (sorbate). Dry of the coat and colour the cheese with annatto solution. Market 2 days later. Mainly matures in 1 month.

Dream of the Abbey (based on Bel Paese) (Chr. Hansen recipe)

Milk	High quality standardised milk is used.	
Heat treatment	Pasteurise at 72°C (162°F) for 15 sec. Cool to 38-43°C (100 – 109°F).	
Culture	Freeze-dried DVS	ST-B01 500 – 1,000u/5,000 litres
	Frozen DVS	ST-BO1 500 –1,000g/5,000 litre
Pre-ripening	30 min at 38 – 43°C	
Rennet	Liquid	NATUREN Standard Plus 175 30–40ml per 100 litres of milk or CHY-MAX Plus 25-35ml per 100 litres of milk
	Powder	CHY-MAX Powder Extra 2.5–3g per 100 litres of milk or NATUREN Standard Plus 900 4–6g per 100 litres of milk
	A gel will form in 30-40 min.	
Cutting	First slowly to obtain a 'thick cut'. After a rest for about 3 min the second cut is continued until a nut dimension is obtained.	
Stirring	10–15 min until the right firmness of the curd is obtained.	
Moulding	The curd is poured into moulds on a draining table and the following acidification takes place in a warm ripening room with high RH 90–95%. The temperature and time vary from dairy to dairy. Some use 24 – 25°C (75 – 77°F) for 6–7 hours, some use 30°C (86°F) for one hour and then 24–25°C (75–77°F), until a pH of 5.2–5.3 is reached. Final acidity 40–45°D. The cheese is turned 4 times during the time in the ripening room.	
Salting	In brine 18-20% NaCl at 15-16°C (59 – 61°F). The time depends on the weight of the cheese. Normally the cheese is salted overnight.	
Ripening	15 – 20 days at 5 – 8°C (41-46°F). RH 85%	
Key figures	24 hours pH	5.2 – 5.3
	Water	44 – 47%
	Fat	28 – 29%
	Salt	2.0 – 2.5

Foxt

John Knox developed this cheese from a recipe provided by Mrs Chester of Townhead Farm.

> *"Dear Mr Knox*
>
> *Cheeses recipe as promised – spelling as in original from Robert Shaw of Townhead farm account book 1860's to 1880's. He died in 1892*
>
> *I come from generations of local farming background. Two of my grandmothers' sisters married cheese factors. Annie married Earnest Green (second wife) he had firstly shop now Indian restaurant corner of Sheep Market/St Edward Street, Leek, and he built the premises known as Pickford's Grocers, corner High Street/St Edward Street, Leek.*
>
> *Mary married Edwin Shirley from Oaken Clough Hall, Longnor, who was a cheese factor and agricultural merchant.*
>
> *Best wishes*
>
> *Christine Chester"*

Cheese Recipe from Townhead Farm, Foxt.

Put the evening and morning milk into a cheese vat and heat together at 84 to 86 degrees with as much rennet or steep as will cause it to come in an hour or an hour and quarter. Break the curd gently and stir it until sufficient whey can be taken off, and heat by placing in a boiler of water to heat the whey in a large milk can

Allow it to heat to 150 degrees but not over. When the whey is nearly hot enough, break the curd, break the curd again as small as possible and keep the curd in motion during the time the hot whey is being poured in and keep stirring until you are quite sure all the curd is equally heated, say five or ten minutes then leave it a sufficient time to settle, say a quarter to half an hour according to the weather

Then lift all together, curd and whey to the drainer. Let it settle for a short time before drawing the whey off. Let the whey drain from the curd until it ceases to run, without putting any weight or whatever on the curd. Then cut the curd up to cool before grinding say 60 degrees if possible

I have omitted to say that if the hot whey heats the curd when poured in and well mixed to 90 or 95 degrees we think it is quite sufficient. I think 7oz of salt to 20lb dry curd sufficient

Robert Shaw, Townhead Farm's Account Book

This cheese won a Bronze Medal at the British Cheese Awards.

Advice from a master cheesemaker

A more recent master cheesemaker from the Staffordshire Moorlands is Dennis Hudson, who shared some valuable advice on his art:

1   The most important thing is to get the acidity right and the correct temperature. "Don't have the acid 'racing' relative to the cheese type," he says, and finally make sure the timing is right.

2   The more fat you put in the cheese the better the quality. "We used to take twin vats and skim the cream off one and put it into the other. This made prize winning cheeses," said Dennis.

3   Old Sage Derby has no sage in. You put a bag of ground sage into a separate small cheese vat and stir in sage colour as acid develops. Make sure you have slow acid development for a good Derby cheese.

Original Derby Cheese was layered as below.

White
Green
White
Green
White

Two green and 3 white is the tradition

Staffordshire Blue

Like most blue cheeses, the Staffordshire Blue was originally made by accident. During the daily turning of cloth bound cheese great care has to be taken to avoid damaging the cheese edges. In some cheese, where the edges had become damaged, airborne mould passed into the mechanical cracks, which are naturally part of the Staffordshire cheese, and the air ingress to the cracks allowed mould to grow.

This cheese had an uneven blueing and although the texture and body were 'yummy' due to the breakdown of the fat and protein, the actual blue flavour was almost non-existent. It was decided to carry out a series of trials based on Stilton method, Shropshire Blue, Caledonian (cheese developed by the West of Scotland Agricultural College), Blue Vinney, Roquefort, Danablu and Gorgonzola to find a better mould distribution and more piquant flavour.

UK Cheese Varieties: Blue veined cheese

Approx. wt. (kg)	Cheese
6 – 8	Blue Stilton, creamy white curd, open texture with blue-green well distributed veins, rough brown coat. (Made at Cropwell Bishop, Melton Mowbray and Hartington)
3 – 5	Blue Wensleydale, creamy white, firm body, open texture, irregular blue veins, coat usually cloth covered.
10 – 20	Blue Cheshire, white or coloured Cheshire type cheese but more acid curds, open texture and blue veining.
10 – 28	Blue Cheddar, well matured, slightly acid Cheddar cheese with blue veining, rarely seen, not usually specially made.
5 – 7	Blue Vinney, rare farmhouse cheese made from hand-skimmed milk, irregular blue veins in a hard cheese body, very piquant when mature. (Made in Dorset from unpasteurised cow's milk. Revived by Mike Davies 1982 - *The World Encyclopedia of Cheese by Juliet Harbutt*)
8 – 10	Staffordshire Blue, creamy white, firm body, open texture, irregular blue veins, cloth covered coat. (John Knox)
3	Lanarkshire Blue made from sheep's milk and the curds are not pressed. Creamy tasting sharp blue cheese flavour with a crumbly texture. (Humphrey Errington)
8 – 10	Shropshire Blue. First made in Scotland, bright orange colour, blue veins, creamy, unpressed, natural rind. (Currently made at Stilton cheese factories)

Manipulation of curds for blue veined cheese

The aim of curd production for blue veined cheese is to produce an acid type of curd with little or no scalding (rarely more than 2°C (36°F)). The manipulation of the curd after breaking or cutting the coagulum is simply to allow slow drainage of the whey after the curd has become firm enough and acid enough in the vat. The draining curds are moved (stirred) sufficiently to prevent pools of free whey forming. When the curd is acid and dry enough it is put into moulds to give it shape. The curds are not generally pressed (Blue Wensleydale is lightly pressed) in order to allow spaces to form between the curd particles in which the blue mould eventually grows. Salt is spread on the surface of the partially dried out curd also to assist drainage of whey. The curd in its mould are turned repeatedly to assist drainage. When the cheese is firm and well drained, it is removed to the ripening store.

The enzymes from the mould growth break down the milk components producing extra piquancy in the cheese flavour. When protein breakdown reaches a certain stage the cheese is pierced by needles to admit air.

The blue of Staffordshire cheese, as previously recorded, was originally made by accident, through the damage of the cloth bound rind during 'turning' during maturation. Good blueing had occurred and so it was obvious that the Staffordshire recipe with its acid open texture was a good medium for mould growth.

The next question was what mould should we add to the cheese to achieve a more piquant flavour and also provide the opportunity for more regular blueing following piercing with stainless steel needles.

Blue veined cheese salting (Scottish Cheese Book)

Salt is usually applied on the curd before moulding, sometimes on the cheese in its mould or indeed after the cheese has been removed from the mould.

Lanarkshire Blue

DV1 starter culture, vegetarian rennet and Penicillium roqueforti are added to the warmed sheep milk. Cut with harp knife, stirred very gently and then curds allowed to settle. Whey drained and soft curds shovelled gently into 3kg moulds and left to drain, no pressing at all. Cheese removed from moulds, brined, and then rubbed all over with salt. Six days later cheese goes to ripening room for 3 months. Stored and pierced vertically. This cheese is made by Humphrey Errington.

Improving Staffordshire Blue

An important fact is that bandaged, pressed Staffordshire cheese still has suitable mechanical fissures in the texture which allow the development of natural mould if the rind is cracked. It was therefore assumed that we could keep to the same make process and simply add Penicillium roqueforti to the milk or curds in order to produce a more piquant flavour and more regular blueing by vertical piercing of the cheese with stainless steel wires at different maturing points. It was also decided to use three sources of the blue mould:

1.   Penicillium roqueforti Alce SRL (liquid)
2.   Penicillium roqueforti Strain vsq (Vis by vac) freeze dried
3.   Penicillium roqueforti Swing PR1 (Chr. Hansen) freeze dried

Two sets of trials were conducted:

4.   Adding Penicillium roqueforti to milk
5.   Adding Penicillium roqueforti to cheese curd after milling and before salting.

Trials	Pierce at 8 days	Pierce at 2 weeks	Pierce at 1 month
1.4			
2.4	There were variable results but adding the Penicillium roqueforti to the milk generally gave a more piquant and regular blueing when piercing was at 7 days following a one month maturing period. Maturing consisted of one week at 4 to 5°C followed by storage at 12 to 14°C until required blueing achieved in up to 4 to 5 months.		
3.4			
1.5			
2.5			
3.5			

The above trial was a practical assessment. The cheese were stored at 14°C and 90 to 85% RH.

It was considered that the blue cheese variety could be further improved by **not pressing** or by **light pressing** by stacking mould on top of one another.

Not pressing

Staffordshire cheese curds were removed to a muslin cloth at the end of stirring period and before running the whey.

The cheese was suspended for 30 mins., removed from the cloth and sliced into pieces which were placed in a stilton mould. Every 2 inch mould was layered across the cheese. When full the mould was turned. Regularly at half hour intervals for 5 hours and then left overnight to drain. Salt was rubbed into the surface of this cheese over a 3 day period. At seven days cheese was vertically pierced and pierced again at 21 days. Inadequate blueing at 8 weeks. This was a one-off trial which needs re-assessing as the texture of the cheese presented interesting possibilities for a superior artisan product

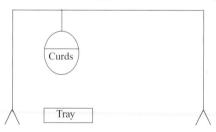

Light pressing

Penicillium roqueforti was added to cheese milk with the starter and the normal Staffordshire Cheese recipe followed. At moulding, cheese was put into 5kg white plastic moulds instead of the 10kg SS moulds. The white moulds were stacked 3 high and moulds changed, in position, every half hour for 3 hours. Cheeses were pierced at 7 days and 21 days. Some blueing and flavour improvement at 10°C and 90 to 95% RH but trials need to be carried out again at storage of 14°C and 90 to 95% RH.

Traditional blue cheese

Pasteurise milk 72°C for 15 secs. (minimum)
Starter 12ml to 100ml/750 litres of milk at 21 to 22°C (no ripening period)
Rennet 25 to 35ml rennet/100 litres milk at 30°C
Cutting 1 to 1.5 hrs vertical knife only 12.5mm (0.5in) blade, lengthways Crossways only sufficient to release whey No horizontal cutting
Pitching No stirring or scalding. Whey is run off the curds when the curd and whey are of equal depth. The curd is then shovelled (plastic food grade or stainless steel shovel) into sinks lined drain trays and left until evening or whey/curd can be run from vat into drainer. In the evening the curds are cut into 15 to 20cm (6 to 8 in) blocks and turned over. The following morning the curd is cut into 10cm (4in) blocks to finish drainage (acidity 1.2%). Repeat breaking or cutting curd to assist drainage if necessary. A peg mill may be used to tear curd and make salt mixing easier and more controllable.
Salting 2.5% dry salt added
Moulding Well mixed salt curd weighed into moulds set on calico cloth on square board – cheese turned daily. Surface of cheese rubbed with palette knife after 3 to 4 days at 4°C and 85% RH.
Ripening 1 After 5 to 9 weeks old curd is mellowed to the stage where blueing will occur if the curd is aerated.
Piercing 10 to 12 holes on each of four sides of the cheese using stainless steel wire at 3mm (0.125in) pierce every week until blueing starts.
Ripening 2 4 to 6 months temperature 18 to 21°C for drying off. 7.2°C after blueing starts

More blue trials

Trials were carried out using Caledonian recipe (similar to Blue d'Auvergne), Gorgonzola, Bresse Bleu.

It was concluded that the Staffordshire Cheese Recipe, with Penicillium roqueforti added to the milk, light pressing. Storage at 4 – 5°C for one week followed by 3 – 5 months storage at 14°C and 90 – 95% RH, followed by piercing at 7-day intervals until blueing starts. Would best serve the milk quality and cheese type of the region.

The main thrust of the blue cheese developments at the Staffordshire Cheese Company Limited was to have a cloth bound lightly pressed cheese to avoid having the cheese coagulum in the vat overnight and the subsequent heavy and laborious turning in the traditional stilton mould.

The next trial will be to place lightly pressed cloth bound cheese in store at 14°C and leave for 14 days and then pierce every week until blueing begins.

What is milk?

Fat

Fat exists in milk as small globules that can vary in size depending on the breed of cow. The fat in the milk helps to produce flavour, aroma and body in mature cheese. Cheese made from skimmed milk is hard in body and texture, and lacks flavour. However, only a small amount of fat (as low as 1%) can produce a background flavour, and today's large manufacturers exploit this with their 'low fat cheese' for which there is a growing demand. This may also be an opportunity for small producers.

Protein

Protein exists in two forms in milk as a suspension/colloidal (casein) and in a soluble form (whey proteins).

When milk sours naturally a fragile curd is formed which collapses with the slightest agitation into tiny fragments. By adding rennet, at just the right time before the milk would go completely sour, the structure of the casein is changed radically to form a solid curd called para-casein. This can then be cut with knives and saved to be collected as curd particles which can be handled to produce a variety of hard cheeses.

Enzymes

In milk different enzymes may arise from the cow herself, from bacteria present in the teat canals or from organisms that gain entry to the milk at a later stage. These enzymes have a profound effect on the quality of the raw milk and the ripening of cheese in store.

Vitamins

These are organic substances in milk which help to promote growth. Milk fat holds the fat soluble vitamins (A, D, E and K) and the water soluble vitamins are the B complex and C which are in the whey. They also play an important part in encouraging bacteria to grow in the cheese ripening process.

Lactose

This is the main sugar in the milk. It provides the energy source for the starter cultures to produce lactic acid, and so helps to modify the milk for cheesemaking.

Ash

Calcium is probably the most important mineral for the coagulation of milk, and together with the protein is an excellent source of food, especially for children who can absorb it quickly into their growth system.

Starter cultures

Starter cultures are harmless micro-organisms used for the fermentation of milk as the first stage in cheesemaking.

In earlier cultures the existence of bacteria and how they worked was not known. The first breakthrough came when the French scientist Louis Pasteur was able to show their harmful effect in wine and later in milk. Lister, an English surgeon, in 1873 isolated a mesophilic bacterium which he named Bacterium Lactis and later known as Streptococcus Lactis (the present designation is Lactococcus Lactis subsp. lactis) for use as a cheese starter culture. In Scotland pure cultures were first used in the South West in 1895. Lloyd in England developed a test to determine the acidity in milk.

Until the middle of the 19th century, cheesemakers on farms simply held over a portion of soured milk or whey in a small jug or churn and used it the following day to make cheese.

Milk must be specially selected for fermentation, e.g. the presence of antibiotics will kill off the starter cultures. The presence of selective bacteriophage will also potentially kill off related cheese starter organisms. Bacteriophage are airborne viruses which are related to the starter cultures used.

Moulds play their part in cheesemaking. The white mould seen on Camembert helps to hydrolyse the protein in the final cheese by working from the outside in. In Stilton manufacture blue moulds can be added with the starter, and help to breakdown the curd produced from the inside of the cheese outwards. Blue cheese is normally pierced with stainless steel wires to let in air which helps the mould to spread and effectively hydrolyse the protein/fat.

Over the last 50-60 years significant work has been carried out in the development of starter cultures within universities and the major cheese companies. Dr Bob Crawford and Janet Galloway carried out significant work at Auchincruive which not only enabled the development of Scottish Mature Cheddar but also continental soft cheeses.

In Unigate Mr James of Ellesmere Creamery carried out work on starter rotations for Cheshire Cheese. The writer followed on with this practical work, at Ellesmere, in the identification of reliable Cheshire starter cultures.

Rennet

Records of the making of rennet go back to the 16th Century. The farmer or smallholder cheesemaker would select and slaughter a milk-fed calf, remove and wash the fourth stomach carefully then hang this out to air-dry in which case it would become known as a 'vell'. It is most likely that dried pieces of vells were added directly to the milk, and at later times vell extracts in salt solution were used.

Rennet is very strong in action (1 part of commercial rennet can coagulate 5,000 parts of milk). The main suppliers are Chr Hansen of Denmark and Rhône Poulenc of France.

Today 'vegetable' rennet is very popular. This is derived from certain strains of fungi and bacteria.

Salt

The salt used in cheesemaking preservation and flavour is sodium chloride, the common salt used at home for cooking and seasoning.

Salt is added to the cheese curd after milling. The purpose is to stop further acid development and provide an element of flavour. The amount of salt varies by cheese type but is around 1.5 to 3.0%. in traditional cheesemaking the salt is added by hand and it is essential to thoroughly distribute the salt evenly over the curds and also mix into the milled curds in an even manner. Failure to do this will result in variable cheese quality.

Typically salted curd cheeses such as Cheddar and territorial cheeses are given overnight pressing.

Cheese may also be salted by floating the cheeses in a brine bath. This is carried out, for example, in Denmark for Havarti, Danbo and other varieties.

Soft cheeses are normally salted by running salt on the outer surface at least once, and sometimes twice. This method of salting also helps to form a rind.

Blue veined cheese salting, where curds are milled, mould may be mixed into the curds after milling and left for one hour before salting.

Moulding and pressing

These are the terms used to define the shape of the salted curds before maturation and sale. In Scotland the traditional cheese mould is called a chisset.

The 4.5kg white food grade plastic mould is normally used for producing rindless wheels which may subsequently be vacuum packed in a food grade plastic bag, waxed or painted with plasticoat to give a rind.

The cloth-lined 8 to 10kg stainless steel mould is used for traditional rinded Cheddar to territorial cheeses. The lined mould and stainless steel follower, shown above, were designed by John Knox for the Staffordshire cheese. The mould was made by local Staffordshire craftsmen.

A cloth-lined square mould is still used in some factories, but the larger units have a Cheddar tower where pressing and compacting of the curd takes place in a continuous flow. These square moulds are used by some small producers to make small round cheeses, especially for Christmas trade. The off-cuts are used in cheese with additives.

Traditional cheese moulds and cheese irons.

Cheese bandaging

There are a number of methods of applying bandages, but the writer prefers to line the mould with a pre-made bag which is hand filled with curds, pre-pressed, taken out of press and the bandage 'pulled up' before capping with a round cloth and finally pressed overnight. The next day the cheeses are 'knocked out' of the mould and 'greased' over all surfaces, using vegetable fat.

Ripening

The writer prefers to make cheese from pasteurised milk with selected cultures for acid and flavour development. Many artisan producers prefer to use raw milk for their cheesemaking, claiming a subtler and richer flavour at the end of the ripening period. There are many great British artisanal cheese made from raw milk. However, with the scientific control and development of cheese starter cultures the writer believes that these traits can be produced in pasteurised milk. He is also concerned about the presence of pathogenic (illness-causing) bacteria in raw milk. Pasteurisation destroys these organisms.

When cheeses are transferred to the maturation room they are date stamped and held at a constant temperature (e.g. 10 to 12°C) to allow uniform ripening and the humidity is carefully controlled to produce the desired moisture content of the ripened cheese without causing excess cheese shrinkage, cracking or undesirable mould growth.

As a result of bacterial and enzymic action during ripening, the cheese will develop its final characteristic texture and flavour. The ripening period is specific to each variety of cheese, e.g. Caerphilly and white Wensleydale may be ready in about two weeks, but a mature Cheddar may take 12 months before being ready for sale.

Adding rennet to ripened milk.

Testing coalgulum before cutting.

Cutting coalgulum with vertical knife.

Checking acidity before running whey.

Whey run off and curds settled on bottom of vat.

Curd handling and 'piling' to control acid and texture development.

Milling the curd ready for salting.

Start to fill traditional cheese mould.   **Filling traditional moulds with curds.**

Cheese grading with cheese iron.

Cheese presentation and sales at British Cheese Awards (marketing assistance from HEFF) .

Pressing cheese in a hand-operated screw press.

Pressing cheese in a horizontal air-operated press.

CHAPTER FOUR

Starter Cultures

 Starter cultures have developed significantly from the "early days" when "sour" milk in a jug was added to the vat. The direct vat entry cultures of today are the essence of cheese acid, texture and flavour development.

In his book "Thought for Food" Nathan Goldenberg of Marks & Spencers said "We were aware from our knowledge of the literature and from discussions with the Scientists at the National Dairy Research Institute, Reading, that cheese made from unpasteurised milk caused food poisoning because of the presence of toxin-producing Staphylococcus Aureus bacteria, this toxin is known to cause sickness and vomiting. To avoid this pasteurised milk must be used. A good deal of opposition was experienced in the trade as it was believed that this would detract from the quality of the final product.

One of the Marks & Spencer cheese suppliers agreed to collaborate with us in a joint commercial scale experiment. A large quantity of milk was divided into two lots; one lot was 'flash' heat treated and the other by full fresh milk pasteurisation. The two lots were made into mature cheddar cheese under exactly the same conditions. The resulting two cheeses were then jointly tested and tasted under code at various stages of maturation. No differences were found in texture, colour or flavour. From that time on all Marks & Spencer cheeses were made from properly pasteurised milk.

The above experiment took place in the 1960's and the writer is even more convinced that with the continued development of starter cultures consistently high quality and flavour cheeses can be made from pasteurised milk. With the added bonus that we are making a safe product.

Starter cultures

A single strain starter is a pure culture, usually of Str. Cremoris or Str. Lactis. It has the advantage that, if satisfactory in vigour and flavour, such a starter can give a steady acid production and thereby a predictable cheesemaking timetable.

Single strain cultures were widely used in Scotland where Dr. Bob Crawford of Auchincruive carried out significant development of these cultures. A disadvantage can be that a single strain is particularly vulnerable to bacteriophage attack and 'dead' cheese may result.

Mixed starters consist of two or more strains, or two or more species, and so may be more variable in behaviour. Mixed starters are safer because if one strain becomes phaged the others can usually continue to work. It has been claimed that mixed starters usually give a fuller flavour than a single strain (Sawicka 1955).

In the Unigate Aston and Ellesmere Cheshire cheese factories a seven day starter rotation was used to avoid the 'dead' vat syndrome created by bacteriophage attack.

The cheesemaking process (Davis 1965) is really a continuation of starter growth in a fresh batch of milk. There is abundant sugar (4.6% lactose initially in the whey) and increasing amounts of soluble nitrogenous compounds resulting from the action of rennet and the bacteria in the milk. Exclusion of air and raised temperatures combine to make cheese curd an extremely favourable medium for starter streptococci, and later for lactobacilli.

A starter, when at its peak (0.7 – 0.8% lactic acid), contains a few thousand million cells per ml as measured by a colony count, and both cheese curd and 'green' cheese (unripened) are almost pure cultures of the starter streptococci if they are properly made (Lloyd 1899, Orla Jensen 1919, Davis 1935).

The larger the inoculum the shorter normally is the lag phase (time to reach desired percentage lactic acid). Historically if a cheesemaker anticipated a weak starter the first thing he/she would do is to increase the amount of starter used.

Modern starters are normally reliable in performance in producing both acid and flavour. A significant potential cause of 'slow' starter is the presence of antibiotics in the milk.

Considerable work was carried out at the Unigate factory in Ellesmere, where 'pairs' of starter cultures were used for Cheshire cheese making. A starter committee was set up to evaluate the practical results of all starter decisions and cultures used. Miss Lillian Stuart, Joe Griffiths, George Higginson, Geoff Spriegel (Secretary and later Technical Director of J Sainsbury) and John Knox (Chairman).

The work of this committee was centred on identifying 'pairs' of starter cultures which would make commercially acceptable Cheshire cheese.

Eleven starter 'pairs' were eventually found after successful vitality tests (see Appendix) and also 'mini' cheesemaking trials in beakers. Since the factory had a bulk starter room it was not possible to make vat size quantities of the tested 'pairs' and when a full vat trial was carried out this came directly after successful laboratory beaker trials. Starter 'pairs' were used and a seven day cycle to avoid potential bacteriophage problems.

Starters for Cheddar making

The texture is firm and close, and the cheese does not crumble when cut. Chr. Hansen recommend their:

Freeze-dried DVS	R-700, R-707 or R-708 500-7—u/5,000 litres RST-744 or RST-776 350-450u/5,000 litres OR
Frozen DVS	R-605, R-607 or R-608 500–750gm/5,000 litres The author has used RST-630 (325-425gm/5,000 litres plus CR-312 5-10gm/100 litres milk to produce excellent mature Cheddar

The make time from renneting to milking is normally 4 hours 30 minutes and pH 5.5 – 5.6

Starters for Wensleydale type cheese

This is a crumbly type cheese. The Staffordshire cheese is a cross between a white Stilton and a Cheshire. John Byng, later Viscount Torrington, noted in his diary that "the cheese of this country pleases me much; being a medium between Cheshire and Stilton" (1790).

The recommended Chr. Hansen culture for this cheese is R-704 at an inoculation rate of 100u per 250 litres. This high inoculation rate is to get a high acidity at a low scald temperature.

Most small scale cheesemakers source their starter cultures from professional laboratories, such as Chr. Hansen, Geest Bricarde, Rhodia Texel, Cargill and others. It is also now the practice with the larger cheesemaking enterprises.

There are exceptions at Davidstow in Cornwall, they manufactured around 17 tonnes of Cheddar Cheese per day in the Tebel Crocket System in the 1970's, but still had their own bulk starter propagation. The Tebel Crocket System was an automated system, used in many of the modern Unigate cheese factories of the period, it still allowed the cheesemaker to 'make the cheese' as the curd handling and salting were still open to view and 'feel'.

The best cheese was said to be made in 4hrs 20min at 0.63% lactic acid. This was a reflection of the good starter performance.

The cheese was stored at 14.5 – 15.5°C (58-60°F) for 2 months before grading.

The modernised Davidstow factory now produces 54 tonnes/day and still has a facility to manufacture bulk starter cultures.

At the Aston Factory traditional Cheshire cheese was made as a cloth bound drum weighing around 10kg.

At Aston mother cultures were stored in liquid nitrogen and from this source sub-cultures (25fl.oz.) were prepared and stored at -20°C until required for inoculation with 9 gallons of pasteurised skimmed milk to form the bulk starter culture.

Preparation of bulk starter

Reconstituted skimmed milk powder (4cwts/300 gallons of water) is weighed in 9 gallon units into churns. The reconstituted skimmed milk in churns is heated by steam in a water tank to 180°F, this takes around 30 minutes. The temperature is thermostatically controlled for one hour. The steam is then turned off and cold water directed into the tank to a temperature of 70-73°F. some 'steaming' takes place to achieve an even 75°F temperature in all churns. A 'dummy' churn containing water is used to regulate temperatures.

The inoculation method devised by John Lewis is used. Churns are aseptically inoculated through a rubber seal which covered in a sterilising liquid.

Half of the churns were inoculated with one strain of starter and half with a second strain. The inoculated churns are incubated for 17 hours. The bulk starter inoculum to the vats (21 gallons of starter/1000 gallons milk) contains both strains of starter organisms in a 50:50 ratio.

The pairing of particular strains is determined by the cheesemaker and laboratory staff following laboratory beaker trials.

Cheshire cheese starter are used in a rotation in an effort to curb the build up of bacteriophage and/or other inhibitory organisms in the cheese room. Particular strains which gave some trouble were rested, whereas those which were totally unsuitable were discontinued permanently.

Within the Staffordshire Cheese Company the cheeses which required special starter cultures were: The Staffordshire, Cheddar, Archie's Choice (crumbly cross between a Stilton and Cheshire), The Abbey Delight (based on Camembert), and Dream of the Abbey (based on Bel Paese).

The Abbey Delight is a Camembert type. Soft, mould-ripened cheese made from cow's milk. Normal cultures used are mixed strain mesophilic. Penicillium candidum is normally used to produce the surface white mould which ripens the fat/protein of the cheese.

Dream of the Abbey is based on Bel Paese, a soft, sweet and milk cheese which was originally produced by Eigidio Galbani in Northern Italy. Bel Paese is a protected Italian name, but the cheese is produced under other names, such as: Italico, Vittoria, Fleur des Alpes and others.

Chr. Hansen recommend their ST-BO1 culture for this cheese at an addition rate of 500–1,000u/5,000 litres of milk for freeze dried DVS or 500–1,000g/5,000 litres of milk for frozen DVS cultures.

Starter preparation

Denaturing the protein by heat assists in the production of a smooth consistency for the cultured starter. Destruction of any resident bacteria in raw milk requires a higher temperature heat treatment than for cheese milks, but for the growth of the starter bacteria, some bands of temperature treatment of the milk are inhibitory and should be avoided.

The temperature band 65–72°C (149–161.6°F) for 30 minutes is stimulatory, as is the band 90-100°C (194–212°F) for 1 to 3 hours. However, a temperature of 120°C (248°F) for longer than 30 minutes is inhibitory, as is the band 72–82°C for 40 – 90 minutes. Heat treatment at 105°C (221°F) is used for the in-bottle or flask sterilisation of milk for laboratory or 'mother' cultures, but the temperature band 90-100°C (194–212°F) is often used for milk in cans or tanks for the preparation of bulk starter for vat use.

Identification of the problem of slow or inactive starter due to bacteriophage, and the necessity for keeping air-borne contamination from milk and growing cultures has resulted in a number of designs for starter milk containers protected by wells containing hypochlorite solution. The John Lewis method is one example.

A sealed, jacketed, insulated tank is now in common use for starter production and normally varies in size between 225 to 4,500 litres (50–100 gallon) depending on the factory requirements, but the heat treatment of the milk, usually by plate heat-exchanger equipment, has varied from flask at 96°C (205°F) to 75°C (167°F) with holding times of 3 to 40 seconds.

Starter propagation

The traditional methods of starter culture propagation begin with a number of laboratory maintained pure cultures whether single strain or mixed strain.

Generally, four to eight such cultures are kept, either as freeze-dried or frozen or liquid cultures. From these cultures, from two to four working laboratory cultures are prepared ready for inoculation and in liquid form these cultures, often termed 'mother' cultures, are tested for 'activity' with regard to acid production and in respect of susceptibility to phage in the cheese milk being used.

The acid activity is the acid produced in milk over a 4-hour period at a temperature of 22–30°C (71–86°F) and acidity produced varies from 0.35% to 0.45% at an incubation temperature of 30°C (86°F). Sometimes a second test is used at a higher incubation temperature 37°C (98.6°F) to indicate growth at scald temperature. A third test is for phage susceptibility.

The 'mother' cultures are then used to inoculate larger quantities of sterile milk. These cultures become the 'factory-mother' cultures. These in turn are used to build up sufficient volume of inoculum for the 'factory' or vat, bulk starter.

Testing is essential on these intermediate cultures. There must be no traffic between factory and laboratory so as to prevent phage being carried into the laboratory.

The simple test for phage in whey consists of inoculating sterile milk with the starter in use, and a small quantity of vat whey. The acidity developed is a measure of phage activity. Sometimes in dye, i.e. resayurin is used instead of acidity measurement. Laboratory tests consist of plating on agar the susceptible bacteria and then spotting whey (or milk) onto the plate. Clear zones indicate phage.

Organisms used in cheese starters

Streptococcus Lactis	A number of strains but avoiding those producing nisin
Streptococcus Cremoris	
Streptococcus Diacetilactis	
Streptococcus Thermosphilus	Withstands higher temperatures
Streptococcus Durans	Grows at higher temperatures
Streptococcus Faecalis	Sometimes used for its flavour producing ability and higher temperature growth
Streptococcus Citrovorus	For flavour production
Streptococcus Paracitrovorus	For flavour production
Leuconostoc Citrovorum	For flavour production
Leuconostoc Dextranicum	For flavour production
Lactobacillus Casei	Used in high scald cheese
Lactobacillus Bulgaricus	Used in high scald cheese
Lactobacillus Helveticum	Used in high scald cheese
Propionibacterium Shermani	Gas and flavour (Emmental)

Development of acidity in milk by a starter

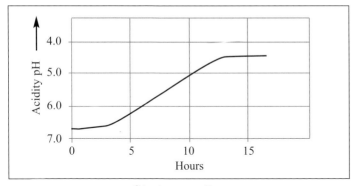

Starter growth

Cheese ripening is the cornerstone in the manufacture of most cheese varieties. It is through ripening that organoleptic characteristic like flavour and consistency are developed controlling the ripening process makes it possible to control the development of flavour and consistency for specific market demands and thereby benefit from branding in an ever increasingly competitive market.

Cheese ripening involves great expenses in the handling and storage of the cheese, which is why any acceleration of the ripening process that does not impair quality of the cheese is of great economic importance.

Specialist cheese laboratories have concentrated their efforts in producing cultures which can be added directly to the cheese milk without disturbing the make process. Chr. Hansen, for example, specialises in composing ripening cultures in collaboration with each individual customer.

Basically ripening is a matter of enzyme activity and many companies have tried to develop enzymes to be added to either the cheese milk or to the cheese curd. Chr. Hansen have developed micro-organisms as sources of supplying the enzymes to be used in controlling cheese ripening. Their effect is only to act as suppliers of a balanced enzyme package. The organisms used have optimum growth temperatures which are very different from the cheese make temperatures and so their activity is virtually nil. It has, therefore, been possible to accelerate the ripening process.

Some cultures used

1.0   CR-Cultures belong to the lactococcus group. This group can be used in cheddar, continental, Emmental and grana. They have strong debittering effect.

2.0   Lactobacillus cultures. Effective as debittering agent. These cultures are used
       in Cheddar, Continental, Emmental and Grana.

       Emfour culture is L. Helveticus and L. Acidophilus. Adding L. Acidophulus
       contributes a fruity, butter like flavour note that may be preferred in continental
       and cheddar cheese varieties.

3.0   Combined ripening cultures

CR-213 + LH-32 - Cheddar	Accelerate ripening and flavour
Emfour + CR312 - Soft (Blue) Grana	improvement

4.0   Surface ripening cultures

Mould is used as the main ripening culture with the production of white and blue
mould cheeses. The mould is strictly aerobic and grows only on the surface of
the cheese. In the blue vein cheeses the mould will also grow in the interior of
the cheese due to the puncturing of the cheese that give aerobic conditions in the
interior of the cheese.

The aerobic conditions open the possibility for oxidative changes during
ripening and the formation of various ketones and keto acids are characteristic
for the flavour of the blue mould ripened cheeses. The moulds possess both
lipolytic and proteolythe activity. This contributes to the characteristic flavour
of the soft cheeses.

White mould cheeses, such as Camembert and Brie, are somewhat different.
The fresh cheese usually has a fairly low pH. The cheeses ripen primarily from
the outside and that is why young Camembert and Brie cheeses possess a hard
center of unripened casein.

A new variety of white mould ripened cheese is the 'stabilised' varieties where
the starter is thermophilic rather than mesophilic. This enables a substantially
longer shelf life for the Camembert or Brie.

5.0   Smear ripening

Many cheese varieties such as Limburger and Tilsiter are surface ripened by
using a so-called smear culture.

In smear ripened cheeses there is a strong symbiosis between the yeast strains
present and the brevibacterium. The yeast initially raises the pH, therefore,
creating optimal conditions for the growth of brevibacteria and micrococcus.

CHAPTER FIVE

The Cheese Market

 **Identifying your target customers and drawing up an effective sales & marketing plan are as important to the success of your project as the quality of your product.**

Some of the most successful cheesemakers in the UK today are carrying on farm-based traditions that stretch back many years. These cheese masters are proud of their farming heritage. Here we take a look at several of the most prominent.

Joseph Heler

The Joseph Heler company is based at Laurels Farm, Nantwich, Cheshire CW 5 7PE (tel. 01270 841500).

Michael Heler reports that his father, Joseph Heler, founded the award-winning Heler business based near Nantwich, in 1957 after attending a cheesemaking course at Reaseheath College, Cheshire. He bought a 700 gallon cheese vat and an old steam boiler. The cheesemaker lived in the attic at the farm.

In 1960 he introduced block-shaped rindless cheese to meet customers' demands. This involved a brave decision, at the time, to stop making cloth-bound cylindrical cheeses.

In 1976/77 pasteurisation of the milk was introduced to meet Environmental Health and major retailer requirements. Enclosed vats were also introduced.

In 1975 there were 70 Cheshire cheesemakers in Chehsire. Now there are only three. Many cheesemakers went out of business because they did not employ a policy of change to meet customer needs. Heler's identify their marvellous success – they now produce 52 tonnes of cheese per day – with a brave investment policy, tears and hard work.

The Heler business is a significant example of a farming organisation focused on progress and profitability.

Lincolnshire Poacher Cheese

This cheese is made by FW Read and Sons, Ulceby Grange, Alford, Lincolnshire LN13 0HE (tel. 01507 466987).

The family's herd of Holstein cows was originally established by the great grandfather of Tim and Simon Jones in 1917. They are the fourth generation in dairy farming.

Tim Jones said that in February 1992 they started to make their Lincolnshire Poacher Cheese which has since won the Supreme Champion award at the British Cheese Awards.

The cheese is a Cheddar type made from unpasteurised Holstein cows' milk. In their make process they use a **chip mill** rather than a **peg mill**, the cheese being made entirely in the vat (and not transferred to a cooler). The curds are "cooked" at a higher temperature than is normal for Cheddar, DVI starters are used for milk ripening. The cheeses are 20kg. in weight and are hot water dipped at 60 – 65°C after leaving the mould, followed by two coats of Plasticoat.

The East Coast grazing, feed and the breed of cows all contribute to the flavour, aroma and texture of this remarkable cheese.

The cheese is a slower make than Cheddar, taking 5½ hours from renneting to milling and matures in around 15 months.

All of their 40,000l/week of milk, from their own herd, is now converted into cheese.

Fowlers Forest Dairies Ltd

Fowlers Forest Dairies Ltd is based at Earlswood, Warwickshire (tel. 01564 702329), from where David Fowler and his wife Pat tell us that the Fowlers are the oldest farm cheesemaking family in Britain. David and Pat are the 13th generation of cheesemakers.

Records show that the family made cheese in 1680 at Hardings Booth, near Buxton in Derbyshire. In 1876 they moved from their Throwley Moor Farm north of Ashbourne, to Hanbury in Worcestershire to be closer to the industrial conurbations and greater outlets for their cheeses.

To this day they continue with the tradition of making Derby Cheeses and have also developed around ten varieties of Warwickshire Cheeses.

They moved to Earlswood in Warwickshire in 1918 and became on-farm milk bottlers and distributors.

In the early 1950s they transferred back to cheesemaking and make 5 tonnes/week of around 12 varieties including Derby Cheeses.

David Fowler's father James developed in-bottle milk pasteurisation. This is still used today for premature baby milk.

Back in 1876, the family's cheesemaking methods threatened to take over the whole farmhouse. A bedroom on the first floor of the farm was made into a cheeseroom – the room's warmth enabling the cheese maturing to progress more quickly. The bedroom window was made into a door and the milk was hauled up to this opening in churns.

Cheese curds wer dropped down to the kitchen for moulding and pressing. Whey from the previous day's make was used as the starter. (What a difference to today's scientifically produced starter strains.)

Some other successful farm-based operations

Some other farmers who have successfully diversified into cheese production are:

(Information from the British Cheese Directory and the World Encyclopedia of Cheese, both edited by Juliet Harbutt)

Charles Martell and Son, who make the famous "Stinking Bishop" and other cheeses.

Appleby's of Hawkstone, who make fabulous Cheshire and Double Gloucester.

Anstey's of Worcester, who make Double Gloucester, Double Worcester and other cheeses of character.

John Alvis of Redhill, Somerset, who makes a significant range of territorials including at least eight organic varieites.

Bath Soft Cheese of Park Farm, Kelston, who make at least four varieties including soft blue.

Colston Basset, Nottinghamshire, who make award-winning blue cheeses of Shropshire and Stilton.

Cropwell Bishop Creamery, Nottinghamshire, who produce award-winning organic Stilton, Shropshire Blue, Stilton and White Stilton.

Dairy Crest of Hartington, Derbyshire, makers of various award-winning blue cheeses including Stilton and Srhopshire Blue

JA & E Montgomery Ltd. Award-winning Cheddar makers.

Mrs Kirkham of Lancashire. Lancashire cheese is a cloth-bound cylindrical cheese made from cow's milk. When mature it is referred to as "Tasty Lancashire". Mrs Kirkham makes one of the finest examples of the latter.

In 2006 the British Cheese Board reported "there are now over 700 different named cheeses being made in the UK alone. The market now stands at 644,000 tonnes. The UK produces almost 400,000 tonnes. The UK market is worth £2.75bn at retail prices".

In the European league table of cheese consumption the UK is near the bottom at around 11kg/person/annum, compared with France, Germany, Italy and Greece who consume more than double this figure.

The British Cheese Board reports "the demand for handmade, high quality speciality cheeses remains strong". They also identify that convenience packaging, 'healthier' cheese, e.g. less fat, less salt or enhanced levels of natural components, e.g. calcium, omega 3. The soft and spreadable cheeses are identified as a specific developing part of the cheese market. See Appendix for details of where to source more information on the cheese market and the cheese industry.

Which bit of the market am I targeting and what does the market want?

Cheese market plans need to consider a number of issues, some of which are:

- do we make organic cheese?
- do we make unpasteurised cheese?
- do we make pasteurised cheese?
- do we make hard cheeses?
- do we make semi-soft cheeses?
- do we make soft cheeses?
- who is going to want to buy my cheese and why?
- what is my key point of difference?
- how and where will I sell the cheese?
- at what price and in competition with which other makers or products?

Potential customers

It is essential to visit all potential sales' outlets in the locality.

- What cheeses do local retailers sell? At what prices?
- Do the pubs and restaurants in the area stock locally produced foods?
- Would these shops and pubs/restaurants be interested in stocking/serving locally made cheese? At what prices?
- If so what types of cheese are they looking for?
- How do all these outlets like the cheese to be packed and in what sizes? What type of volumes might they be interested in?
- What delivery frequency and shelf life are they looking for?
- Payment terms should be cash on delivery

Answering all of the above questions help to guide you to what type of cheese you should be making and helping to identify the potential size of the market. Further assistance can be gained from the local marketing initiatives sponsored by Food from Britain, the Local Business Link, Rural Hub, the Milk Development Council and other local agencies. Initially farmers do not normally look to sell through major retailers until they have established their products and gained some track record in successful local sales. Major retailers will require at least British Retail Consortium Certification before trading with a food business.

In general, success will depend on having a product that:

- is demonstrably local

- is different in some way from mainstream cheeses found in supermarkets

- has a distinctive appearance and flavour and is seen as good value for money as a speciality rather than an every day cheese (the intention being, it is suggested, to be able to retail the cheese at a price well above £10 per kg).

In setting up a cheese business the farmer producer can normally cope with attending eight farmers' markets per month and cheese deliveries to local farm shops, delicatessens, pubs and restaurants. This is based on two staff having involvement in cheesemaking, say three days per week followed by cutting and packaging into retail portions of say 2kg, 1kg, 200 – 300gms. Preparing products for the farmers' markets, selling and post market cheese handling are time consuming and tiring work. However, as one farmer noted "John, if you had to milk cows twice/day you would know what work was!"

The business plan needs to be regularly discussed and changed as appropriate. Good quality marketing data is essential (see Appendix). The Staffordshire Cheese Company had promotion in local press, magazines and with leaflets produced by HEFF (Heart of England Fine Foods). These leaflets were of a high quality and helped considerably with the image and promotion of our hand crafted products.

The farmers' market stall needs thought and design. We had banners publicising our name, our products and our awards. The banner was 3ft (9km) deep and 80 inches (203cm) long with gold lettering on a black background. This made it easy for customers to see us and provided excellent cheese publicity.

After one year of 8 markets per month we recruited part-time staff trained them in the cheese room and cheese types and then set them to sell at additional farmers' markets. This made a considerable improvement to our turnover and profitability. Besides providing excellent financial returns the farmers' market gives you the priceless experience of talking directly to your customers and making product and range changes as necessary.

There are many sources of business, sales and marketing assistance for Staffordshire cheesemakers: Business Link, Heart of England Fine Foods, Specialist Cheesemakers' Association, British Cheese Awards, Rural Hub, Milk Development Council and The British Cheese Board.

The Staffordshire Cheese Company joined the Specialist Cheesemakers' Association and Heart of England Fine Foods (part of the Food From Britain Marketing Initiative). These two organisations give substantial and cost-effective services in developing different areas of your cheese business.

Labelling

It is important to check the label design and other cheese pack information with the Trading Standards Officer before progressing to the printing stage.

In 2001, following the dreadful Foot and Mouth problems, the countryside was shut down for several months. The Business Link made available my great friend Max King who came along to help me make a 'Recovery Plan'.

At this time 79% of the cheese market was in multiple retailers, such as M & S, Sainsbury, Tesco, Asda, Waitrose, and Morrisons. 8% of the market was co-operatives, 4% independents such as Budgens and Spar and finally 9% in specialists/farm/delicatessens. The latter was our market at this stage.

According to Mintel the cheese market in 2001 was worth £1.4bn. We estimated that the total cheese market in Staffordshire was £20m, a 1% market share (ignoring sales to any other county) would give us a market potential of £200,000 per year. This together with a 0.1% market share of the market in the adjacent counties of Cheshire, Derbyshire, Shropshire, Greater Manchester, as well as the enormous potential in London and the South East, would give an additional market potential of some £500,000 per year and so we estimated our minimum market recovery size to be £700,000 per year.

In June 2001 we reviewed our position, in view of the total closure of the countryside from March 2001 due to Foot and Mouth Disease.

Our main marketing routes were:
- Farmers' markets
- Specialist shops
- Pubs and restaurants

We also attended major food fairs at Arley Hall Manchester, Chester Agricultural Show, Shugborough Hall Food Exhibitions, Food Shows at the NEC in Birmingham and Food Events at various London locations.

We joined the Heart of England Fine Foods (HEFF) who are part of the Food From Britain marketing initiative. They helped us with publicity, marketing data, low cost attendance at major food events and the networking opportunities with other regional food producers.

We also joined the Specialist Cheesemaking Association which gave us considerable value in terms of networking, technical information, appropriate HACCP to meet new legislation and also the contact with Juliet Harbutt of the British Cheese Awards. At The British Cheese Awards we gained Silver and Bronze awards for our cheeses and tremendous publicity with all areas of the retail and specialist cheese buying trade.

In 1998 we had also won 1st Prize for our Archie's Choice cheese at the Bakewell Show.

In order to recover from FMD we decided to produce goats' milk cheese and also a semi-soft cheese to add diversity to our range and increase our sales potential. Our range was now to be:

The Staffordshire	Cloth bound
Staffordshire Blue	Cloth bound
Archie's Choice (AC) (Bronze medal)	Black waxed
Archie's Vintage Rindless	
Moorlander Oak Smoked	Rindless. AC smoked over burning oakwood
Captain Smith's Titanic	Curds washed in real ale
The Abbey Beer & Garlic (Silver medal)	Cloth bound. Curds washed in ale and mixed with garlic
Cheddleton with Chives	4 week old rindless cheese mixed with chives

The Abbey Delight	Similar to a Camembert in shape, finish and texture
Dream of the Abbey	Based on Bel Paese
Foxt (Bronze Medal)	A cloth bound, 4kg round cheese based on a cheesemaking recipe used at Townhead Farm, Foxt, Staffordshire
Rudyard (Bronze Medal)	A cloth bound hard goats' cheese based on the Staffordshire Cheese recipe
Longsdon	Soft goat cheese based on Port de Salut

These cheeses were designed to give our recovery plan (after FMD) a major forward thrust.

We also developed regional sales with co-operatives, but were not relaxed about being involved with multiple retailers. Our policy for increased sales still focussed on more farmers' markets, farm shops, pubs and restaurants and we decided to also focus on other regional groups, such as Booths in Lancashire, Budgens and Spar.

However, to really move the business forward, within our own control, the author decided that a local farm shop and distribution centre, owned by the producers, offered a significant way forward. (See Chapter 7)

CHAPTER SIX

Business Plan

 **Drawing up a detailed and realistic Business Plan, taking into account all the likely costs over at least a four-year priod, is a vital step at the outset of cheesemaking.**

It is essential to consider a Business Plan before investing in any type of food production, especially cheese.

In the book by Janet Arthur 'Say Cheese' 1870 – 1970, she says "Cheese was heavy work, done by women. During the summer most of the day would be occupied in making cheese and turning those already made. The cheese matured slowly and was sold at annual cheese fairs, although some buyers visited the farms to pick choice quality". Artisan cheese making is still long and heavy work and selling the product into local venues is time consuming.

In the Staffordshire Cheese Company, John Knox and his son, Simon, started work at 7am and finished by 4pm with all cheese to press and the necessary cleaning and hygiene completed. Cheese was made three times per week with two days on cheese grading, packing and product development. The final two days in the week were devoted to selling at various farmers' markets and delivering to local farm shops, hotels, restaurants and pubs. These selling activities covered all costs of production, bank charges, wages and a small profit. The profitability was enhanced when part-time staff were employed for specific sales targets and also when regional stores and selected retail outlets stocked our product.

Rachel Bridge reported in the Sunday Times, October 2006, "the first farmers' market opened in Bath in 1997; nine years later there are more than 500 certified farmers' markets across the country".

Markets typically run for 3 to 5 hours at a weekend, weekly or monthly depending on the size of the local population. Customers spend £166m a year at them. Most farmers' markets charge £25 a market stall. London has a range of markets attended by cheesemakers from as far away as Cheshire and Lancashire.

Considerable help to build your business plan is available from Specialist Cheese Consultants, Business Link, Milk Development Council, Rural Hub, Food from Britain (which has regional marketing groups such as The Heart of England Fine Foods, North

West Fine Foods, Taste of the West and others) and The Specialist Cheesemakers Association.

In looking at a Business Plan it is essential to consider such issues as food miles, organic or non-organic, hard cheese or soft cheese, pasteurised milk or raw milk cheeses, potential sales and marketing outside of the normal regional area. It is recommended that at least four varieties of cheese are considered for the Business Plan development. This gives a 'cheese board' and the opportunity for increased sales over a single variety, e.g. restaurants require more than one variety of cheese for their cheese board.

Some cheese types which can be considered:

Cheddar, Wensleydale, Port Salut, Camembert, Bel Paese, Feta, Blue Cheese Types and other territorial or continental cheeses.

The following marketing and business plans are based on a hard cheese type.

The first issue for the cheesemaker / owner is to ensure that all basic running costs, bank repayments and wages can be met. Direct sales at farmers' markets, local farm shops, delicatessens, pubs and restaurants offers the opportunity to achieve this when a focussed approach is applied to developing sales through these outlets.

The emphasis is on selling hand-made, traceable, artisanal cheeses of quality and distinction.

The sales and marketing plan is based on increasing sales through the above outlets over the period of the plan (4 years) and selling into regional retail stores and selected multiple retailers, e.g. Waitrose, from year 2.

The plan becomes the focus for corrective action and business development. To achieve these sales additional part-time sales staff are required for farmers' markets and deliveries. It is also recommended that additional sales management input comes from relevant sales consultants and cheese mongers, who are paid on a results basis.

Getting the product quality and presentation correct is the first priority. It is recommended that hard cheeses are always cloth bound to give them a traditional hand-made look.

Summary of Plan

Year 1 - Investment £12,450 sales £33,225
Cumulative Cash Balance at year end £5,160
Year 2 - sales £38,476 Cumulative cash balance - £14,260
Year 3 - sales £60,002 Cumulative cash balance £25,329

Year 4 - sales £97,358 Cumulative cash balance £40,296

Note 1: This sales, marketing and business plan is based on a Territorial type hard cheese with a minimum yield of 9.3 litres of milk per one kilogram of cheese.

Note 2: In year 1 Dairy Technology Consultancy costs of £3,750 is included in the overheads. This assumes that a Business Link Listed Consultant is used with a 50% financial assistance. This cost includes the development of the HACCP.

Note 3: The target sales in year 4 are 10.5 tonnes per annum.

Fowlers Farmhouse Cheese sell 400 tonnes per year

Lynher Dairies Cheese Company sell 36 tonnes per year

North Bradon Farmhouse Cheese sell 10,000 tonnes per year

Shepherd's Purse Farm Cheese sell 60 tonnes per year

Note 4: The cheese sold at Farmers' markets is costed at £14.60/kg, which the writer achieved in 2004. Some cheesemakers may sell at £12.50/kg or less for the same product, this is a matter of judgment for individual cheesemakers. In a speciality cheese shop(November 2006) in London cheeses were on sale for £17.00/kg to £25.95/kg for speciality cheeses. Study of a website for speciality cheese showed £550gms traditional cloth-bound cheese, from the West Country, on sale for £12.50 excluding delivery.(November 2006)

Note 5: The room size is 20ft by 15ft and the costing of £12,500 assumes that the farmer will source and manage his own room conversion with help from a suitably qualified consultant. This room size is suitable for a start-up situation.

It would be very easy for these costs to escalate to much higher levels if the work was completely sub-contracted by the farmer.

Some farmers may wish to start with a much larger facility to accommodate future developments. The writer set up a 2,000sq.ft. facility following a smaller scale start-up of the size indicated above. The larger facility cost £30,000 to build and equipment costs were £33,700.

Some farmers have quoted small cheese room costs as high as £96,000, but this is where work was mainly subcontracted and the most expensive prices paid for building materials.

SALES / EXPENDITURE / CASHFLOW FORECAST FOR YEAR ENDING 31st March 2007

Month -	April	May	June	July	August	September	October	November	December	January	February	March	Total	Cost per Kg
SALES														
Farmers Mkts - Kg	60	70	70	70	80	80	100	110	130	60	80	90	1,000	
Farmers Mkt - £ (@£14.50)	870	1,015	1,015	1,015	1,160	1,160	1,450	1,595	1,885	870	1,160	1,305	14,500	
Farm Shops - Kgs	20	15	15	20	30	40	50	50	60	25	30	30	385	
Farm Shops £ (@7.50)	150	113	113	150	225	300	375	375	450	188	225	225	2,888	
Other sales - Kgs	10	10	15	15	15	20	20	40	40	20	20	20	245	
Other Sales - £ (@£7.50)	75	75	113	113	113	150	150	300	300	150	150	150	1,838	
Total Sales - Kgs	90	95	100	105	125	140	170	200	230	105	130	140	1,630	
Total Sales	**1,095**	**1,203**	**1,240**	**1,278**	**1,498**	**1,610**	**1,975**	**2,270**	**2,635**	**1,208**	**1,535**	**1,680**	**19,225**	**£11.79**
EXPENDITURE														
PURCHASES														
Milk	151	159	168	176	209	235	285	335	385	176	218	235	2,730	
Cultures	7	8	8	8	10	11	14	16	18	8	10	11	130	
Packaging, labels, boxes	32	33	35	37	44	49	60	70	81	37	46	49	571	
Total Direct Costs	**189**	**200**	**211**	**221**	**263**	**295**	**358**	**421**	**484**	**221**	**274**	**295**	**3,431**	**£2.11**
OVERHEADS														
Wages	80	80	80	80	80	80	80	80	80	80	80	80	960	
Telephone	25	25	25	25	25	25	25	25	25	25	25	25	300	
Postage & Stationery	80					40							120	
Transport	50	50	50	50	50	50	50	50	50	50	50	50	600	
Contingency Costs	20	20	30	30	30	30	30	50	50	30	30	30	380	
Professional Fees											250		250	
Consultancy Costs		2,000		750		750		250					3,750	
Heat, Light and Power	50	50	50	50	50	50	50	50	50	50	50		550	
Finance and Bank Charges	250	250	250	250	250	250	250	250	250	250	250	250	3,000	
Depreciation	150	150	150	150	150	150	150	150	150	150	150	150	1,800	
Total overheads	**705**	**2,625**	**635**	**1,385**	**635**	**1,425**	**635**	**905**	**655**	**635**	**885**	**585**	**11,710**	**£7.18**
CASHFLOW														
Inflow														
Sales receipts	1,095	1,203	1,240	1,278	1,498	1,610	1,975	2,270	2,635	1,208	1,535	1,680	19,225	
Loans														
Capital Introduced	14,000												14,000	
Total Receipts	**15,095**	**1,203**	**1,240**	**1,278**	**1,498**	**1,610**	**1,975**	**2,270**	**2,635**	**1,208**	**1,535**	**1,680**	**33,225**	
Outflow														
Purchases	189	200	211	221	263	295	358	421	484	221	274	295	3,431	
Overheads	705	2,625	635	1,385	635	1,425	635	905	655	635	885	585	11,710	
Capital equipment	12,500												12,500	
Total Payments	**13,394**	**2,825**	**846**	**1,606**	**898**	**1,720**	**993**	**1,326**	**1,139**	**856**	**1,159**	**880**	**27,641**	
Monthly in/out/flow	1,701	-1,622	395	-329	599	-110	982	944	1,496	351	376	376		
Balance b/f	0	1,701	78	473	144	743	634	1,616	2,560	4,056	4,407	4,784		
Cum. in/outflow	**1,701**	**78**	**473**	**144**	**743**	**634**	**1,616**	**2,560**	**4,056**	**4,407**	**4,784**	**5,160**		

SALES / EXPENDITURE / CASHFLOW FORECAST FOR YEAR ENDING 31st March 2008

Month:-	April	May	June	July	August	September	October	November	December	January	February	March	Total	Cost per Kg
SALES														
Farmers Mkts - Kg	90	105	105	105	120	120	160	180	180	90	120	135	1,510	
Farmers Mkt - £ (@£14.60)	1,314	1,533	1,533	1,533	1,752	1,752	2,336	2,628	2,628	1,314	1,752	1,971	22,046	
Farm Shops - Kgs	25	25	25	25	35	45	60	70	70	30	35	35	480	
Farm Shops £ (@7.60)	190	190	190	190	266	342	456	532	532	228	266	266	3,648	
Other sales - Kgs	10	10	15	15	15	20	20	40	40	20	20	20	245	
Other Sales - £ (@£7.60)	76	76	114	114	114	152	152	304	304	152	152	152	1,862	
Retail Shop/Agents - Kgs	100	100	100	100	120	120	200	200	200	100	110	110	1,560	
Retail Shop/Agents - £ (@ £7.00)	700	700	700	700	840	840	1,400	1,400	1,400	700	770	770	10,920	
Total Sales - Kgs	225	240	245	245	290	305	440	490	490	240	285	300	3,795	
Total Sales	1,580	1,799	1,837	1,837	2,132	2,246	2,944	3,464	3,464	1,694	2,170	2,389	38,476	£10.14
EXPENDITURE														
PURCHASES														
Milk	377	402	410	410	486	511	737	821	821	402	477	503	6,831	
Cultures	18	19	20	20	23	24	35	39	39	19	23	24	304	
Packaging, labels, boxes	79	84	86	86	102	107	154	172	172	84	100	105	1,328	
Total Direct Costs	474	505	516	516	610	642	926	1,031	1,031	505	600	632	8,463	£2.23
OVERHEADS														
Wages	120	120	120	120	120	120	120	120	120	120	120	120	1,440	
Telephone	25	25	25	25	25	25	25	25	25	25	25	25	300	
Postage & Stationery	80			80		40	80			80			360	
Transport	100	100	100	100	100	100	100	100	100	100	100	100	1,200	
Contingency Costs	40	40	40	40	40	40	40	40	40	40	40	40	480	
Professional Fees			500										500	
Consultancy Costs												250	250	
Heat, Light and Power	100	100	100	100	100	100	100	100	100	100	100	100	1,200	
Finance and Bank Charges	250	250	250	250	250	250	250	250	250	250	250	250	3,000	
Depreciation	150	150	150	150	150	150	150	150	150	150	150	150	1,800	
Total overheads	865	785	1,285	865	785	825	865	785	785	865	785	1,035	10,530	£2.77
CASHFLOW														
Inflow														
Sales receipts	1,580	1,799	1,837	1,837	2,132	2,246	2,944	3,464	3,464	1,694	2,170	2,389	27,556	
Loans													0	
Capital Introduced													0	
Total Receipts	1,580	1,799	1,837	1,837	2,132	2,246	2,944	3,464	3,464	1,694	2,170	2,389	27,556	
Outflow														
Purchases	474	505	516	516	610	642	926	1,031	1,031	505	600	632	7,988	
Overheads	865	785	1,285	865	785	825	865	785	785	865	785	1,035	10,530	
Capital equipment													0	
Total Payments	1,339	1,290	1,801	1,381	1,395	1,467	1,791	1,816	1,816	1,370	1,385	1,667	18,518	
Monthly in(out)flow	241	509	36	456	737	779	1,153	1,648	1,648	324	785	785		
Balance b/f	5,160	5,401	5,910	5,946	6,403	7,139	7,918	9,071	10,719	12,366	12,690	13,475	5,160	
Cum. in(out)flow	5,401	5,910	5,946	6,403	7,139	7,918	9,071	10,719	12,366	12,690	13,475	14,260	14,260	

SALES / EXPENDITURE / CASHFLOW FORECAST FOR YEAR ENDING 31st March 2009

Month	April	May	June	July	August	September	October	November	December	January	February	March	Total	Cost per Kg
SALES														
Farmers Mkts - Kg	130	130	130	150	150	150	220	250	250	140	140	160	2,010	
Farmers Mkt - £ (@£14.60)	1,898	1,898	1,898	2,190	2,190	2,336	3,212	3,650	3,650	2,044	2,044	2,336	29,346	
Farm Shops - Kgs	40	40	40	40	40	50	60	70	70	40	40	40	570	
Farm Shops £ (@£7.60)	304	304	304	304	304	380	456	532	532	304	304	304	4,332	
Other sales - Kgs	20	20	20	20	20	20	20	20	20	20	20	20	240	
Other Sales - £ (@£7.60)	152	152	152	152	152	152	152	152	152	152	152	152	1,824	
Retail Shop/Agents - Kgs	250	250	250	250	250	300	350	400	450	250	250	250	3,500	
Retail Shop/Agents - £ (@ £7.00)	1,750	1,750	1,750	1,750	1,750	2,100	2,450	2,800	3,150	1,750	1,750	1,750	24,500	
Total Sales - Kgs	440	440	440	460	460	530	650	740	790	450	450	470	6,320	
Total Sales	2,354	2,354	2,354	2,646	2,646	2,868	3,820	4,334	4,334	2,500	2,500	2,792	60,002	£9.49
EXPENDITURE														
PURCHASES														
Milk	737	737	737	771	771	888	1,089	1,240	1,323	754	754	787	11,376	
Cultures	35	35	35	37	37	42	52	59	63	36	36	38	506	
Packaging, labels, boxes	154	154	154	161	161	186	228	259	277	158	158	165	2,212	
Total Direct Costs	926	926	926	968	968	1,116	1,368	1,558	1,663	947	947	989	14,094	£2.23
OVERHEADS														
Wages	200	200	200	200	200	200	200	200	200	200	200	200	2,400	
Telephone	25	25	25	25	25	25	25	25	25	25	25	25	300	
Postage & Stationery	80		80		80		80		80		80		480	
Transport	125	125	125	125	125	125	125	125	125	125	125	125	1,500	
Contingency Costs	50	50	50	50	50	50	50	50	50	50	50	50	600	
Professional Fees												250	250	
Consultancy Costs													0	
Heat, Light and Power	60	60	60	60	60	60	60	60	60	60	60	60	720	
Finance and Bank Charges	250	250	250	250	250	250	250	250	250	250	250	250	3,000	
Depreciation	150	150	150	150	150	150	150	150	150	150	150	150	1,800	
Total overheads	940	860	940	860	940	860	940	860	940	860	940	1,110	11,050	£1.75
CASHFLOW														
Inflow														
Sales receipts	2,354	2,354	2,354	2,646	2,646	2,868	3,820	4,334	4,334	2,500	2,500	2,792	35,502	
Loans													0	
Capital Introduced														
Total Receipts	2,354	2,354	2,354	2,646	2,646	2,868	3,820	4,334	4,334	2,500	2,500	2,792	35,502	
Outflow														
Purchases	926	926	926	968	968	1,116	1,368	1,558	1,663	947	947	989	13,304	
Overheads	940	860	940	860	940	860	940	860	940	860	940	1,110	11,050	
Capital equipment													0	
Total Payments	1,866	1,786	1,866	1,828	1,908	1,976	2,308	2,418	2,603	1,807	1,887	2,099	24,354	
Monthly in(out)flow	488	568	488	818	738	892	1,512	1,916	1,731	693	613	613		
Balance b/f	14,260	14,748	15,316	15,803	16,621	17,359	18,251	19,763	21,679	23,410	24,103	24,716		
Cum. in(out)flow	14,748	15,316	15,803	16,621	17,359	18,251	19,763	21,679	23,410	24,103	24,716	25,329		

SALES / EXPENDITURE / CASHFLOW FORECAST FOR YEAR ENDING 31st March 2010

Month:-	April	May	June	July	August	September	October	November	December	January	February	March	Total	Cost per Kg
SALES														
Farmers Mkts - Kg	200	200	230	230	230	250	320	350	350	220	220	220	3,020	
Farmers Mkt - £ (@£14.60)	2,920	2,920	3,358	3,358	3,358	3,650	4,672	5,110	5,110	3,212	3,212	3,212	44,092	
Farm Shops - Kgs	40	40	40	40	40	50	60	70	70	40	40	40	570	
Farm Shops £ (@7.60)	304	304	304	304	304	380	456	532	532	304	304	304	4,332	
Other sales - Kgs	20	20	20	20	20	20	20	20	20	20	20	20	240	
Other Sales - £ (@£7.60)	152	152	152	152	152	152	152	152	152	152	152	152	1,824	
Retail Shop/Agents - Kgs	500	500	500	500	500	580	700	750	750	450	500	500	6,730	
Retail Shop/Agents - £ (@ £7.00)	3,500	3,500	3,500	3,500	3,500	4,060	4,900	5,250	5,250	3,150	3,500	3,500	47,110	
Total Sales - Kgs	760	760	790	790	790	900	1,100	1,190	1,190	730	780	780	10,560	
Total Sales	**3,376**	**3,376**	**3,814**	**3,814**	**3,814**	**4,182**	**5,280**	**5,794**	**5,794**	**3,668**	**3,668**	**3,668**	**97,358**	**£9.22**
EXPENDITURE														
PURCHASES														
Milk	1,273	1,273	1,323	1,323	1,323	1,508	1,843	1,993	1,993	1,223	1,307	1,307	19,008	
Cultures	61	61	63	63	63	72	88	95	95	58	62	62	845	
Packaging, labels, boxes	266	266	277	277	277	315	385	417	417	256	273	273	3,696	
Total Direct Costs	**1,600**	**1,600**	**1,663**	**1,663**	**1,663**	**1,895**	**2,316**	**2,505**	**2,505**	**1,537**	**1,642**	**1,642**	**23,549**	**£2.23**
OVERHEADS														
Wages	300	300	300	300	300	300	300	300	300	300	300	300	3,600	
Telephone	40	40	40	40	40	40	40	40	40	40	40	40	480	
Postage & Stationery	80		80	80	80		80		80		80		480	
Transport	200	200	200	200	200	200	200	200	200	200	200	200	2,400	
Contingency Costs	50	50	50	50	50	50	50	50	50	50	50	50	600	
Professional Fees													0	
Consultancy Costs														
Heat, Light and Power	80	80	80	80	80	80	80	80	80	80	80	80	960	
Finance and Bank Charges	250	250	250	250	250	250	250	250	250	250	250	250	3,000	
Depreciation	150	150	150	150	150	150	150	150	150	150	150	150	1,800	
Total overheads	**1,150**	**1,070**	**1,150**	**1,070**	**1,150**	**1,070**	**1,150**	**1,070**	**1,150**	**1,070**	**1,150**	**1,320**	**13,570**	**£1.29**
CASHFLOW														
Inflow														
Sales receipts	3,376	3,376	3,814	3,814	3,814	4,182	5,280	5,794	5,794	3,668	3,668	3,668	50,248	
Loans														
Capital Introduced													0	
Total Receipts	**3,376**	**3,376**	**3,814**	**3,814**	**3,814**	**4,182**	**5,280**	**5,794**	**5,794**	**3,668**	**3,668**	**3,668**	**50,248**	
Outflow														
Purchases	1,600	1,600	1,663	1,663	1,663	1,895	2,316	2,505	2,505	1,537	1,642	1,642	22,229	
Overheads	1,150	1,070	1,150	1,070	1,150	1,070	1,150	1,070	1,150	1,070	1,150	1,320	13,570	
Capital equipment													0	
Total Payments	**2,750**	**2,670**	**2,813**	**2,733**	**2,813**	**2,965**	**3,466**	**3,575**	**3,655**	**2,607**	**2,792**	**2,962**	**35,799**	
Monthly in(out)flow	626	706	1,001	1,081	1,001	1,218	1,815	2,219	2,139	1,061	876	876		
Balance b/f	25,329	25,955	26,661	27,662	28,744	29,745	30,962	32,777	34,996	37,135	38,196	39,072		
Cum. in(out)flow	25,955	26,661	27,662	28,744	29,745	30,962	32,777	34,996	37,135	38,196	39,072	39,948		

Cheese manufacturing room

In starting a cheese business it is recommended that investment be kept to a minimum at the beginning for two reasons:

1.   You might start making cheese and discover you do not like the work (is it possible that someone would not like making cheese?)

2.   Keeping investment as low as possible at the start gives the optimum opportunity to make a profit from the enterprise.

The Staffordshire Cheese Company Limited started in a small enterprise unit at Knutton, Newcastle under Lyme. The approximate unit size was 20ft by 15ft. This was rented on a monthly basis from the Business Innovation Centre, Stafford, making it easy to move on when appropriate sales had been realised.

The capital investment in plant and buildings was based on the minimum start-up investment. A 750 litre capacity raw milk storage tank was converted into a batch pasteuriser/cheese vat by removing the ice-block equipment and replacing it with heating elements to facilitate batch pasteurisation and also water flows to achieve the starter inoculation temperature of approximately 30°C.

When considering an appropriate building and equipment the Environmental Health Officer should be involved at the earliest stages to assist in this process.

Capital costs

Cheese vat conversion	£2,500.00
Cheese press	£1,500.00
Cheese cutting knife	£200.00
Small cheese mill	£1,000.00
Traditional moulds (7)	£700.00
Stainless steel table	£250.00
Sink for equipment washing	£500.00
Hands free sink	£500.00
Maturing room	£2,750.00
Refrigerator for retail cheese sales	£500.00
Special floor and walls	£1,250.00
Scale	£500.00
Ancillary (thermometer etc.)	£300.00
TOTAL	**£12,450.00**

Room size

A room of 20ft x 15ft would be an approximate size for housing the above equipment. Our maturing room was a modified refrigerated delivery wagon.

Sales/cheese production

In the costing data given in this plan

    4 farmers' markets are attended per month in year 1
    6 farmers' markets are attended per month in year 2
    8 farmers' markets are attended per month in year 3
    12 farmers' markets are attended per month in year 4

Within two years the writer had his cheese at 16 farmers' markets per month and selling direct to the public at maximum financial return gave sufficient cash flow to pay all bills and wages with a small profit. Sales to the other outlets of farmers' market shops, delicatessens, pubs, hotels and restaurants provided additional margin.

Manpower requirements to meet sales plan (based on 50 weeks)

YEAR 1

Total cheese sales	1632kg
Weekly cheese sales	32.64 kg
Manpower weekly	1 day cheesemaking
	1 day cheese handling and cutting/packing for market
	1 day at farmers' markets
	= 3 man-days

Note: Assumed that cheeses will be delivered to shops and restaurants during farmers' market journeys.

YEAR 2

Total cheese sales	4752kg
Weekly cheese sales	95 kg
Manpower weekly	1 day cheesemaking
	1 day cheese handling and cutting/packing for market
	1 day at farmers' market per 2 weeks and 2 days at farmers' markets per 2 weeks
	= 3 man-days for 2 weeks and 4 man-days for 2 weeks

YEAR 3

Total cheese sales	6672kg
Weekly cheese sales	133 kg
Manpower weekly	2 day cheesemaking
	1.5 day cheese handling and cutting/packing for market
	2 days at farmers' market per week
	= 5.5 man-days

YEAR 4

Total cheese sales	10,560kg
Weekly cheese sales	211 kg
Manpower weekly	3 day cheesemaking
	3 day cheese handling and cutting/packing for market
	3 days at farmers' market per week
	= 9 man-days

Note 1: The writer used a group of ladies to sell at the 16 farmers' markets. They were each given cheesemaking training over a two day period before being allowed to attend a market. The first market was accompanied by the cheesemaker to show how to sell the cheese and explain the cheese make, cheese profiles and other details.

Note 2: Cheesemaking is a very physical and demanding activity. It requires considerable enthusiasm and dedication to achieve consistently high quality results.

The above 750 litre vat and equipment can accommodate the achievement of the 4 year plan, which is detailed above. This plan is achievable for any farmer who is focussed and enthusiastic about developing added value cheeses. With additional sales consultancy help from the beginning of the business it is possible to achieve even higher sales and margins.

After one year The Staffordshire Cheese Company moved to a 2,000 sq.ft. unit at Cheddleton near Leek, Staffordshire.

The Staffordshire Cheese Company dairy 1999

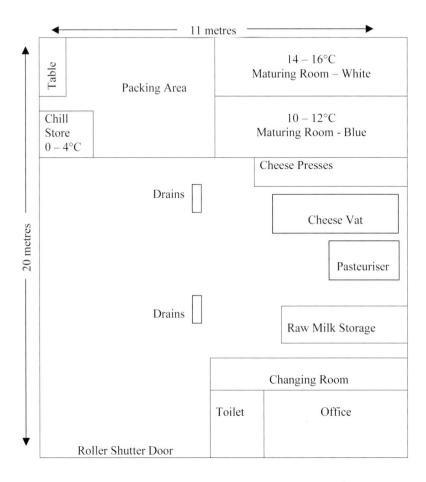

Room costs

With project control by the cheesemaker or the farmer it is possible to set up a new unit of 2000 sq.ft. including roof, support steel and impervious, easy to clean Kingspan panels and epoxy resin floor for £30,000. The steel and roof, outer protection sheets and epoxy resin floor would all be new. The cost of the panels is based on sourcing good quality second hand materials, which is not difficult. Some cheesemakers and farmers have been able to buy panels from larger food businesses which are rationalising production into a smaller number of factories. Other good buys are second hand 'hands free' sinks, lighting and test equipment. Most second hand equipment is reliable, but it is recommended that you never buy a second hand steam boiler as these are known to be a source of serious problems.

Floors to be sloped to drains. This is very important to ensure satisfactory drainage of vat rinses, floor cleaning and detergents. Free water on the floor can be a source of microbiological problems.

Selection of the floors is a fundamental issue. It is recommended that floor tiles are not used as they can be damaged by 'chipping' and then present the possibility of debris getting under the tiles presenting a possible microbiological problem or floor securing problem. Never paint food floors, it is an expensive waste of time. Normal wear and small milk or hot detergent spillages will soon remove the paint.

A non-slip epoxy floor is needed. Flortex EP (Tel. 01234 840740) will report that correct laying and after it is fully cured (7 to 14 days) the floor will withstand caustic solution at temperatures up to 85°C and is also unaffected by milk. The floor cost is £3,000. other floor types are Flowcrete HF (Tel. 0958 774018) and Flo Dek Ltd (Tel. 01902 380334). All floor areas need to be coved at base of wall to ensure effective cleaning.

Light fittings need to be protected so that any glass breakage does not result in glass getting into cheese.

Cheesemaking equipment for 2,000 litres/day of hard cheese

Cheese vat

Convert farm milk tank into a batch pasteuriser/cheese vat £2,500.00. A 2,000 litre cheese vat can cost £10,000.00 minimum with no stirring equipment. Converting a farm milk tank is a good starting point until you have sufficient turnover and profit to justify say a cheese vat and curd tray. The latter takes away the 'back breaking' job of leaning over the vat during 'cheddaring' of hard cheese varieties.

Press for hard cheese

• A twin horizontal cheese press with air-compressor and 2 press pistons can be easily made at a cost of £2,500.00.

• Old vertical hand operated presses can still be found and these can cost up to £400 each. The capacity of these presses depends on cheese size. They will take 8 x 5kg cheeses or 4 x 10kg cheeses. 2,000 litres of milk = 200kg (min) of cheese, that is 5 presses x £400 = £2,000.00.

Both pneumatic and hand operated presses allow the flexibility for different pressing levels depending on the cheese type being made.

Cutting knives

The knives are called American Knives and are designed to cut the coagulum vertically and horizontally.

The distance between the blades is critical to achieving the correct cut size in the coagulum, e.g. Wensleydale will be walnut size pieces, whereas Cheddar will be the size of peas.

For hard cheese manufacture $^{1}/_{4}$" between the blades is generally recommended.

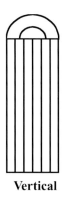

Vertical

Horizontal

Mill

An electronically operated pin mill will tear the curds leaving lots of surface area for the salt to be effectively mixed. Cost £3,000.

It is possible to consider having a hand operated mill fabricated by local stainless steel manufacturers, but this is only recommended for start up volumes of around 50kg of cheese.

Moulds

Moulds give shape to the cheese and also allow whey drainage.

Plastic moulds are now popular for soft cheeses and 4.5kg wheels whereas larger cheeses normally have stainless steel moulds.

To achieve a traditional round cheese of 8 to 15kg it may be necessary to design the mould and have it made by a stainless steel fabricator.

Cost of 10kg SS moulds are around £80.00 each

Cost of 4.5kg plastic moulds

Cost of small moulds for soft cheeses

Maturing rooms (10 to 12°C)

In hard cheese maturation a temperature of 10 to 12°C will give suitable opportunity for continued bacterial growth and cheese flavour/texture development.

Blue cheese can be matured at 12 to 14°C and a relative humidity (RH) of 85 to 95%.

Soft cheeses, such as Camembert, can be matured at 11 to 13°C and 90 to 95% RH for 3 to 4 weeks.

A maturing room (10 to 12°C) can be set up, with good quality second hand Kingspan panels and refrigeration for around £1,500.

Chill room (0 – 5°C)

A chill room is necessary, particularly for soft cheeses, but normally retail cheese for farmers' markets is packed in portions and stored in chill store before going to market. Cost of store around £1,500.

Ancillary costs

• 2 stainless steel tables for preparing moulds, cutting cheese and 'greasing' traditional cheeses. Cost around £400.00.
• Plastic wash sink for moulds, knives and other pieces of equipment £250.00
• Hands free sink £300.00
• Scales £500 (labels handwritten to start)
• Audimeter, thermometer, cheese iron, knife for cutting cheese curd (hard cheese production) £150.00

Total cost for setting up hard cheese production = £32,600.00

CHAPTER SEVEN

Farmers' Market Shop
and Distribution Centre

 **The right sales and distribution channel is important to any artisanal food producer. This chapter details plans for a dedicated Farmers' Market Shop and Distribution Centre.**

One of the biggest problems for small food producers is the marketing, selling and distribution of products. The products are made with great care and real ingredients, however individual artisans are often so caught up in the quality and dedication to detail that it leaves little time – outside of farmers' markets and local sales to farm shops, restaurants, pubs and delicatessens – for the producer to full develop sales.

As a solution to this sales and marketing challenge, the author developed detailed plans for a Farmers' Market Shop and Distribution Centre in Leek. Selling high quality, locally produced speciality food products direct to the consumer, the premises would also act as a centre for distributing artisan food and drink to other retail outlets and catering establishments, and be supported by a e-commerce website offering a home delivery service.

Such a scheme could be replicated in many parts of the country, delivering key benefits to artisanal food producers including:

• the opportunity to increase sales at reasonable profit levels and within an ethos of low food miles

• customer involvement in knowing their food producer and food history, and

• having a shop and distribution centre which share their values.

In the case of the Leek shop, it was proposed to finance the project by selling shares in a Limited Company totalling £60,000 to investors from the local rural community, matched by grant funding of £72,000. A Board of Directors were to be recruited from the investors with a specialist food manager appointed to run the shop and distribution centre. The shop's turnover was estimated at £240,000 in Year 1 rising to £491,000 in Year 5.

With a project of this scale, professionally qualified consultants would be able to offer advice on the key elements of the plan: raising finance, retailing and distribution, quality management and marketing.

Market background

The UK food retail market is dominated by the top four supermarkets, who hold a combined 70% market share. However, the growing trend towards 'farm produced' food enables smaller retailers to differentiate their products from the supermarkets' mainstream products.

Initiatives such as food fairs organised by Heart of England Fine Foods have increased awareness of locally produced foods. Additionally, the Foot and Mouth crisis of 2001 and previous BSE problems created major concern for food safety amounts consumers. The desire for safe, traceable food continues to grow.

A Mintel survey conducted in 2001 found that:
- 73% of consumers were concerned about meat safety
- 2 out of 3 were aware of increasing use of additives
- Food allergies were on the increase
- Health and fitness regimes were extensive
- World travel changes consumers' outlook on food
- Organic foods have changed public perceptions

Target customers

The target customers of a Farmers' Market Shop and Distribution Centre can be divided into two sectors:

The Public:

Such a shop would target local retail consumers within the socio-economic groups A, B and C1. The lifestyles of these groups make them less likely than the national average to cook more than three times per week at home. However, they use high quality ingredients and host more dinner parties than other social classes.

Tourist visitors looking for local produce/souvenirs would be another segment of the market.

The more affluent members of society tend to purchase from major supermarkets en route to work and during normal commuting time. They are more likely to seek, both offline and online, more specialised foods if they are entertaining and are therefore another target group.

Businesses:

The shop's distribution facility could target the hospitality sector (local pubs, hotels, restaurants, tea shops), local tourist sites and other farm shops.

Key issues

Important issues which need to be considered include:
- Locality: heartland / outland
- Hinterland density / trading / catchment area
- Store location and suitability.
- Traffic flow
- Competition from multiples and local stores
- Store size and staffing levels
- Staff competence / procedural disciplines

The vital first step of such an enterprise is to build local support and create demand from consumers. It's important to create a modern approachable store which would sell as wide a range of products as possible. The aim should be to add value at every opportunity.

Marketing

A local Farmers' Market Shop will not compete with multiple retailers on price, although value for money would be a key attribute of the products sold. It would compete on the basis of higher quality goods sold at a price which reflects that quality. Purchases already appreciate that organic foods attract a premium price and are willing to accept such a premium. The growth of the organic food market and vegetarian markets have already successfully educated and influenced more affluent members of society to pay premium prices.

Competitive advantage would be gained through a strategy of making this shop different from its competitors by emphasising key features:
- Locally produced goods with a farm guarantee
- Products sourced from small suppliers, maintaining the exclusivity of the outlet
- High quality produce and 'best practice' Quality Management System
- Friendly approach and detailed supplier and product knowledge

A detailed and well-researched marketing strategy would play a key part in its success A pro-active programme of marketing activities would
- help to establish the outlet
- create local and regional awareness
- attract trade business
- gain a regular, continuing and growing customer base.

Typical elements of the marketing programme would be:
- consistent branding
- production and distribution of leaflets
- direct mail
- PR in local and regional media,
- advertising in the local press and radio
- launch of a company website, both for publicity and to facilitate online ordering
- other marketing materials including car stickers and point of sale material

1.   The company

1.1   History of the company

Leek Farmers Market Shop (LFMS) has been formed to facilitate a new distribution channel for farm producers with Leek and the surrounding areas of Staffordshire. It will be a limited company, which will be for the benefit of producers. It is anticipated that these producers will be the Company's shareholders. A retail unit and distribution centre will be established within the Leek area where farm produce will be sold, marketed, order picked and distributed.

The retail unit will consist of a high-class shop with a traditional authentic ambience. Both the retail unit and distribution facility will be capable of selling fresh, chilled and frozen produce.

It is intended that the distribution centre will be aimed at business customers wishing to take artisan food and drink purchases for resale in retail outlets or for use within catering establishments.

A steering group was formed in January 2002 and currently has the following membership:
- John Knox (Cheesemaker and previously the Manufacturing Director of Kerrygold in Leek)
- Jill Norman (Staffordshire Moorlands District Council)

This steering group is responsible for establishing the strategic direction of the organisation and overseeing the performance of the Shop/Stock Manager that will be appointed.

1.2   Company vision and objectives

The Steering Group's vision for the Company is for it to become the market leader within the Staffordshire Moorlands and surrounding area for the retail distribution of farm produce via a farm shop environment.

In order to measure progress towards achieving this vision, the following short-term objectives have been defined:

• Turnover of £240k in Year 2, £344k in Year 2, £370k in Year 3, £441k in Year 4 and £491k in Year 5

• To achieve a net profit of £15k in Year 2 and £16k in Year 3, £28k in Year 4 and £36k in Year 5

• To raise loan funding in Year 1 of £60k through farm investors

• To raise grant funding of £71.32k in Year 1

1.3 The industry

The UK food retail market is dominated by the top four supermarkets, who hold a combined 70% market share. However, there is a growing trend towards 'farm produced' food, which can enable smaller retailers to differentiate their products from the supermarkets mainstream products.

Many major retailers have attempted to establish 'farm produced' food sourcing initiatives, including Sainsbury, Morrisons and Safeway. "Food from Britain" has also set up 'farm produced' initiatives. For example, Heart of England Fine Foods (HEFF) to specifically assist local producers. HEFF have arranged food fairs, "meet the buyer" and other initiatives, which have increased awareness of locally produced food.

The Foot and Mouth crisis of 2001 and previous BSE problems have created a major concern for food safety and within the UK customers have also become concerned at the food control in major retailers. There is a continued growth in consumer need for safe, traceable food.

2. Products and services

2.1 Current products

A full range of farm produce will be sold by the organisation including:

• Cheeses

• Meats

• Poultry

• Jams, preserves, oils etc.

• Vegetables

• Eggs, Bread, Biscuits

- Wines
- Others (including craft sales)

2.2 New product/service development

If successful, the LFMS model will be offered to organisations within other regions of the Country. This will provide LFMS with the opportunity to provide consultancy services to help other organisations establish their operational and marketing infrastructure.

The product range that is to be offered will be surveyed to establish which products are no longer desired by consumers and new additions to the range will be researched.

3. Markets

3.1 Market size

The populations of the areas from which LFMS will attract its customers are as follows:

Area	Population 000's
Staffordshire Moorlands	95
Staffordshire	809
Manchester	2,573
Derbyshire	947
Cheshire	967

The financial projections reflect the seasonality of the market, which has been based upon work carried out by the Farm Retailers Association.

3.2 Customers

The target customers can be divided into two sectors, as follows:

Public

The shop will target local retail consumers within the socio-economic groups A, B, and C1. The lifestyles of these groups make them less likely than the national average to cook more than three times per week at home. However, they use high quality ingredients and host more dinner parties than other social classes.

Tourist visitors looking for local produce/souvenirs will also be targeted. It is anticipated that they will have similar characteristics to the local retail customers described above.

The more affluent members of society tend to purchase from major supermarkets en route to work and during normal commuting time if travelling by car. They are more likely to seek, both offline and online, more specialised foods if they are entertaining and are therefore a likely target audience. If they have access to the Internet at their workplace, they are more likely to use breaks to surf the Internet and will make purchases using this medium.

Business

The distribution facility will target the hospitality sector (local pubs, hotels, restaurants, tea shops), local tourist sites and other farm shops. However, the financial projections do not provide for any sales to this sector.

3.3 Competitors

The company will compete with other market shops and specialist food suppliers. However, within Leek and the surrounding area there are no direct competitors offering the same proposition as Leek Farmers Market Shop. It is this uniqueness which is detailed in 4.1 that will enable the company to gain a competitive advantage over other local food retailers.

The company will seek to develop an e-commerce site that provides a delivery service of specialist food products. There will be competing sites for this type of activity and the company will carry out a competitive analysis prior to launching its site to ensure that it is able to position itself to gain a competitive advantage.

4. Marketing

4.1 Unique selling points

Leek Farmers Market Shop will not compete with multiple retailers on price, although value for money will be a key attribute of the products sold. LFMS will attempt to obtain a competitive advantage through a strategy of differentiating itself from its competitors. The following differentiating features will be emphasised in the marketing of LFMS:

- Locally produced goods, with a farm guarantee
- Products are sourced from small suppliers, maintaining exclusivity to LFMS
- High quality produce and 'best practice' Quality Management System
- Friendly approach and detailed supplier and product knowledge

4.2 Marketing methods

The following methods will be used to promote the company's products:

• The shopping experience provided by the shop ambiance

• A direct mail campaign to business customers will be undertaken upon the launch of the distribution facility and regular mailshots will also be undertaken. This will be complemented by regular telesales promotions.

• LFMS will subscribe to the Heart of England Fine Foods organisation as a source of region-wide marketing and professional assistance.

• A PR programme will be pursued across local press and magazines and a wider national forum. This will include a 'first brick to first birthday' concept.

• A company website will be launched that facilitates online ordering.

• Other marketing methods such as leaflets, car stickers and point of sale material will also be undertaken.

4.3 Pricing policy

The company accepts that it cannot compete with supermarkets on price and will not attempt to do so. It will compete on the basis of higher quality goods and the price of goods offered by LFMS will reflect this quality.

Purchasers already appreciate that organic foods attract a premium price and are willing to accept such a premium. The growth of the organic food market and vegetarian markets have already successfully educated and influenced the more affluent members of society to pay premium prices.

4.4 Distribution policy

LFMS will use the following channels to distribute its products:

• A retail site in Leek town centre

• A distribution centre near to Leek, which will service both the retail shop and business customers. The site will also service personal orders for food hampers ordered online or via the shop for home delivery.

• A website will be developed that will facilitate online ordering.

5.0 Operations and location

5.1 Supplies

It has been agreed by the Steering Group that all sourced products must meet specific criteria, including:

• All products must be produced by the supplier.

- All suppliers must be approved by LFMS. The evaluation will be based upon the perceived risk to the consumer.
- A limited number of suppliers will exist for each product category, for example meat, cheese, poultry.
- Initially only packaged and labelled meats will be sourced. This will avoid the need to comply with the special regulations relating to butchers shops.

The suppliers will be sourced from Staffordshire, Cheshire, West Midlands, Derbyshire, Nottinghamshire, and Greater Manchester.

5.2   Premises and equipment

A retail shop will be acquired on a leasehold basis in, or close to, Leek town centre. A distribution centre, with the facility to store chilled and frozen foods, will also be established nearby. Planning permission for the premises will be sought when suitable premises have been identified.

5.3   Quality control procedures

John Knox Ltd are specialists in Quality Control and would develop the necessary supplier approvals, food legislative controls, quality assurance manual, work instructions and quality control records necessary for the Company to implement a robust quality control system.

6.   Management and staff

6.1   Shareholders

The equity shares of the Company will be issued after the investors have been identified. It is anticipated that the equity finance, and associated shareholders loans, and the DEFRA grant will be reliant upon each other.

6.2   Directors and staff

John Knox will be a director of the Company and the initial Company Secretary. Other non-executive directors will be appointed when the above shareholdings have been finalised.

An experienced Supply Chain Manager will be appointed to oversee the operations of the organisation. It is anticipated that an ideal candidate would be a retired supermarket manager. The role of this manager has been defined as follows:

'To manage the day-to-day operation and staff of a retail outlet selling farm produce. To assist in meeting LFMS commercial objectives and maximising the opportunities to promote local farm produce.' To help identify further business opportunities within this retail development a job description has been included in Appendix 4.

A salary of £25,000 has been included within the financial projections for the Shop and Supply Chain Manager in Year 1. It has been provided that this will increase by £1,000 per annum and also include a bonus system based on sales performance over the agreed budget.

A Supply Chain Assistant(s) has been included at a cost of £6,000 per annum.

Director's fees of £1,000 per month have been included within the financial projections.

6.3   Management Information Systems

To ensure that the directors have sufficient, relevant information to assist them with decision-making, reports will be produced, including:

- Monthly management accounts
- Other financial teports (including cash flow and profit projections)
- Product profitability analysis
- Customer complaints log

6.4   Training policies

Only experienced staff will be recruited and in depth training will be provided to ensure that the staff employed are fulfilling their potential. This will include the following:

-        Company induction
-        Food and hygiene training
-        Customer knowledge
-        Product knowledge
-        Customer service/complaints handling
-        Code of conduct (e.g. dress code, attitude, shopping experience)

7.   Contingency plans

The directors have identified the following risks and their respective contingency plans:

7.1 Sales volumes being lower than forecast

In these circumstances, the company's marketing strategy would be overhauled. The company would utilise its product profitability analysis to discontinue with some product ranges and would carry out market research to establish what they should be replaced with. Other distribution methods, such as focussing on e-tailing or business-to-business sales, would be considered.

7.2 Failure to secure DEFRA grant

In these circumstances, the business would not be able to proceed and the project would be abandoned.

7.3 Unsuitable goods being received from a supplier

John Knox has a network of farming contacts, which will make it possible to replace any supplier who provides unsuitable produce. All suppliers will be regularly evaluated, to measure the level of quality being provided.

8. Funding requirements

Financial projections have been prepared with assistance from PKF, which have confirmed the following funding needs:

Share capital

The company will be formed with an issued share capital of £100.

Directors' loans

The company will seek loan investment from shareholders in proportion to their shareholdings. This has been included within the financial projections at £60,000.

DEFRA Rural Enterprise Scheme (RES) Grant

The financial projections provide for an RES grant of £71,320, which will enable the Company to launch its retail unit and distribution facility. Without this grant support, the project will not be able to proceed.

9.   Financial summary

9.1   Growth

The projected growth of the company can be summarised as follows:

	2004/5	2005/6	2006/7	2007/8	2008/9
	£	£	£	£	£
Sales	240,700	344,350	370,000	441,000	491,000
Cost of Sales	162,672	232,508	249,790	297,576	331,288
Gross Profit	78,028	111,842	120,210	143,424	159,712
	32%	32%	32%	32%	32%
Overheads & Depreciation	129,497	111,181	114,853	118,106	120,736
Operating Profit	(51,469)	661	5,357	25,318	38,976
RES Grant	17,830	14,372	10,780	8,084	6,064
Net Profit	(33,639)	15,033	16,137	33,402	45,040
Corporation Tax	0	0	0	4,950	9,008
Retained Profits	(33,639)	15,033	16,137	28,452	36,032
Retained Profits B/fwd	0	(33,639)	(18,606)	(2,469)	25,983
Retained Profits C/fwd	(33,639)	(18,606)	(2,469)	25,983	62,015

Profit and loss account

The Balance sheet of the company during the period of the forecasts can be summarised as follows. The opening balance sheet has been prepared from information supplied by the directors.

Balance sheet

	2005	2006	2007	2008	2009
	£	£	£	£	£
Fixed Assets	61,334	48,668	38,402	30,720	24,576
Current Assets	45,083	67,640	83,574	119,659	162,695
	106,417	116,308	121,976	150,379	187,271
Current Liabilities	26,466	31,696	32,007	40,042	46,966
Long Term Liabilities	113,490	103,118	92,338	84,254	78,190
Net Worth	(33,539)	(18,506)	(2,369)	26,083	62,115
Share Capital	100	100	100	100	100
Retained Profits	(33,639)	(18,606)	(2,469)	25,983	62,015
	(33,539)	(18,506)	(2,369)	26,083	62,115

The projected cash flow of the company can be summarised as follows:

	2004/5 £	2005/6 £	2006/7 £	2007/8 £	2008/9 £
Balance B/fwd	0	36,236	58,536	74,460	158,321
Loan Funding	60,000	0	0	0	0
Share Issue	100	0	0	0	0
RES Grant	71,320	4,000	0	0	0
Trading Receipts	300,430	404,635	434,772	518,180	576,922
Payments	395,614	386,335	418,848	434,319	452,398
Balance C/fwd	36,236	58,536	74,460	158,321	282,845
Peak Balance	55,298	58,536	91,008	164,076	282,845
Lowest Balance	7,976	31,260	48,872	71,259	156,572

CHAPTER EIGHT

HACCP - Hazards, critical control points and microbiology

 **A HACCP is needed by law (EU Regulation 852/2004, article 5), but it is also essential to ensuring safe food production. The food law requirements keep changing and the Specialist Cheesemakers' Association and Dairy UK keep cheesemakers up to date with current requirements.**

1.0 Dairy Farming Control at the farm

The Dairy Inspectorate of the Food Standards Agency visit the dairy farm once/year to audit the dairy farm methods, milking of cows and plant cleaning.

Dairy farm records of drugs, animal husbandry, calving records, cleaning procedures are all controlled to the requirements of 'Milk Hygiene on the Dairy Farm', a practical guide for milk producers to the Food Hygiene (England) Regulations 852/853/854 – 2004, prepared by the Dairy Hygiene Inspectorate of the Food Standards Agency.

We purchased our milk from dairy farmers of Britain, who also monitored farm performance and, in particular, milk hygiene and composition.

2.0 Cheesemaking Control

2.1   In order to manufacture cheese an Application for Approval of a Food Business Establishment subject to approval under Regulation (EC) No. 853/2004 has to be completed and sent to the local #Environmental Health Officer for evaluation.

2.2   A.5.65 Appendix B – Guidance on documents to be provided by an establishment in advance of Approval (see Appendix) also needs to be completed to send with 2.1 above.

2.3   Microbiological standards for milk and milk products has to be arranged in accordance with Summary 2006 – Testing to be carried out by dairies under EC Reg. 853/2005 and 2073/2005 (see Appendix).

2.4   In preparing a cheesemaking HACCP our Environmental Health Officer recommended that we take due note of 'Milk Hygiene' Regulations for Dairy Product Processors prepared by the Ministry of Agriculture, Fisheries and Food, Department of Health, Welsh Office, Scottish Office DAN1/DHSS N1. Contents in appendices.

2.5   In A.5.56 Appendix B it is recorded that "the documented food safety management system should show the hazard analysis for each process (or process group where appropriate, i.e. in small businesses), and include details of how the proposed critical points were established and validated, including the results of any sampling, and the proposed monitoring and control arrangements".

2.6   The original HACCP developed for the Staffordshire Cheese Co. is based on the Dairy Industry Federation guidelines for Hygienic Practice in the Manufacture of Dairy-Based Products May 1995

These guidelines give immediate identification to the Critical Control Points which is so important, particularly in small scale manufacture with limited staff resources.

2.7   The Food Standards Agency in co-operation with The Specialist Cheesemakers' Association, ADAS and LACOTS produced a Food Safety Workbook for the Manufacture of Cheese. This workbook was designed to assist specialist cheesemakers with limited experience in developing a HACCP. An ADAS consultant and the local Environmental Health Officer were required to complete the workbook with the specialist cheesemaker.

The Staffordshire Cheese Company also completed this workbook and received the appropriate certificate of completion.

The workbook is copyright of the Food Standards Agency.

3. Staffordshire Cheese Company – Generic flow diagram for Hard Pressed Cheese

(Based on Dairy Industry Federation – Guidelines for Hygienic Practice in the Manufacture of Dairy-based Products May 1995)

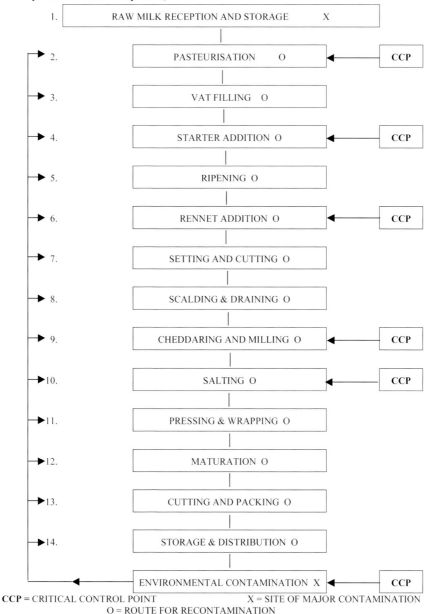

1. RAW MILK RECEPTION AND STORAGE   X

2. PASTEURISATION   O   ◄———— CCP

3. VAT FILLING   O

4. STARTER ADDITION O   ◄———— CCP

5. RIPENING O

6. RENNET ADDITION O   ◄———— CCP

7. SETTING AND CUTTING O

8. SCALDING & DRAINING O

9. CHEDDARING AND MILLING O   ◄———— CCP

10. SALTING O   ◄———— CCP

11. PRESSING & WRAPPING O

12. MATURATION O

13. CUTTING AND PACKING O

14. STORAGE & DISTRIBUTION O

ENVIRONMENTAL CONTAMINATION X   ◄———— CCP

CCP = CRITICAL CONTROL POINT   X = SITE OF MAJOR CONTAMINATION
O = ROUTE FOR RECONTAMINATION

4.   Hard Pressed Cheese

4.1   Process and Hazard Analysis

Hard pressed cheeses, when manufactured and handled according to good manufacturing practice, do not present any significant risk to the consumer with respect to pathogenic micro-organisms or their toxins. Microbiological stability (preservation) is afforded by the acidity (reduced pH) and reduced water activity of hard pressed cheeses.

Food poisoning incidents involving hard pressed cheese have usually involved toxins of Staphylococcus aureus or contamination by salmonellae. For both of these pathogens and for other pathogens it is demonstrated that growth will not occur and, in fact, the contaminating micro-organisms will die out as the cheese matures, providing acid development in the vat and during ripening is normal.

However, if acid development is retarded due to poor starter activity or bacteriophage attack or antibiotics in milk, contaminating pathogens can multiply in the vat and during pressing and numbers can survive throughout maturation. In outbreaks involving hard pressed cheese with Staphylococcus aureus toxins and salmonellae, investigations have attributed failure to inadequate acid production and poor plant hygiene.

The following sub-paragraphs correspond to the fourteen steps in the generic flow diagram overleaf and indicate the hazards and control measures relevant to hard pressed cheese manufacture.

4.1.1   Raw milk and storage

The **hazards** associated with **reception** is that raw milk will, on occasions, contain pathogenic bacteria. Thus, a hazard is introduced onto the processing site.

Assuming no post-pasteurisation contamination, the consumer will be protected by three **control measures**:-

-        the pasteurisation process given to milk;

-        the design of the processing site itself, which should ensure that contamination from the raw side to the finished product side does not occur;

-        management of personnel, so as to ensure that there is no 'cross-over' from raw to finished areas without adequate hygienic steps being applied.

The **hazard** associated with **storage** is that bacterial multiplications will occur, including:-

- pathogenic bacteria which can cross-contaminate other process areas;
- spoilage bacteria which may cause taints, such as lipolytic rancidity;
- Additionally, raw milk may contain inhibitory substances, such as antibiotics, which might impair ripening.

Control measures include:-

- appropriate raw milk specification, identification, traceability and testing;
- defined temperature and time storage conditions. The milk should be maintained below 5°C and the time in the storage limited to a maximum of 48 hours before pasteurisation;
- if the milk is to be used within 2 hours of milking the cow, it may be used directly without cooling;
- raw milk handling is at the opposite end of the process from the cheese vat;
- defined cleaning and barrier hygiene rules.

4.1.2   Pasteurisation

This is the most important **control measure**.

The **hazard** is that milk, if not pasteurised correctly, will allow the survival of pathogenic bacteria which may grow to large numbers and/or produce toxins, especially during the fermentation period.

The **control measure** is ensuring that the milk is heated at 71.7°C for 15 seconds (or equivalent). This is achieved by correct design and running of pasteurising plant. Thermometers measure the temperature, which is continually recorded, and flow rate controls determine the holding time. A flow diversion valve ensures that raw milk, which has not reached the correct temperature, will be returned to the raw milk balance tank. Should diversion occur, it must be ensured that raw milk has not contaminated the pasteurised milk side of the plant. If contamination has occurred, the plant will be cleaned and disinfected before re-use. Verification of the correct functioning of the diversion valve will be carried out daily.

In addition, a pressure differential between the raw milk side and the pasteurised milk side is in operation, such that if any leaks occur it is from pasteurised back to raw.

The process presents the following **hazards**:-

-    failure to reach correct temperatures;
-    failure to reach correct holding time;
-    recontamination of pasteurised milk by plate leaks in regeneration sections.

Control measures to apply include:-

-    the use of process equipment to maintain the required temperature with flow diversion devices to reject milk not heated to that temperature;
-    correct holding tube to give minimum hold time at maximum possible throughput;
-    maintenance of positive pressure differential between process and raw milk side in regeneration sections;
-    instrument calibration;
-    regular, scheduled checks of plates for leakage.

Verification of pasteurisation to be carried out by testing processed milk for phosphatase activity and Coliforms.

4.1.3   Vat filling

The filling of cheese vats with pasteurised milk presents one main **hazard**:-

-    recontamination from poorly cleaned lines and surfaces (microbiological effect of C.I.P. residues).

Control measures to apply include:-

-    defined and scheduled cleaning procedures.

4.1.4   Addition of starter culture

This process stage presents the following **hazards**:-

-    introduction of microbiological contaminants with starter as supplied;
-    contamination during handling of additions;
-    wrong addition rates.

Control measures include:

-    effective supplier quality assurance through specification and audit;

\-   appropriate operator work instructions to ensure hygienic handling and correct addition rates.

4.1.5   Ripening

The **hazard** to consider here is:-

\-   contamination during sampling and testing.

Control measures include:-

\-   normally only titrable acid test will be conducted and care is to be taken to ensure that test equipment is hygienic.

4.1.6   Rennet addition

This process stage presents the following **hazards**:-

\-   introduction of microbiological contaminants with rennet as supplied;

\-   contamination during handling or addition;

\-   wrong addition rate.

Control measures include:-

\-   effective supplier quality assurance through specification and audit;

\-   hygienic handling and correct addition rates using specific measuring cylinder.

4.1.7   Setting and cutting

The **hazards** to consider here are:-

\-   contamination during sampling and testing;

\-   recontamination from poorly cleaned lines and surfaces (microbiological or C.I.P. residues).

Control measures include:

\-   ensure hygienic sampling and testing;

\-   defined and scheduled cleaning procedures.

4.1.8   Scalding and draining

The **hazards** to consider here are:-

\-   contamination during sampling and testing.

Control measures include:-

- ensure hygienic sampling and testing;
- defined and scheduled cleaning procedures.

4.1.9   Cheddaring and milling

Fermentation is a key critical control point.

The **hazards** to consider here are:-

- the pasteurised milk may be contaminated with pathogenic bacteria, either through failure of control steps 1-1.8 or by recontamination from equipment or factory environment, which could include transfer of raw milk contaminants;
- slow or failed starter activity which results in the milk remaining at a high pH for sufficient time to allow contaminants to grow to unacceptable levels.

Control measures include:-

- defined and scheduled cleaning procedures for both equipment and factory environment;
- use of an active starter culture at the correct addition rate and chosen to be resistant to local bacteriophage types;
- defined barrier hygiene rules to avoid cross-contamination between raw milk and other high hazard areas and in the cheese room environment.

Monitoring the rate and level of acidity development is critically measured at milling or just prior to salting.

Where acidity development fails to achieve a titratable acidity of 0.4% lactic acid within 6 hours of (vat fill) pasteurisation, then **corrective action** will be to reject or to quarantine for additional tests before release.

4.1.10   Salting

The **hazards** to consider here are:-

- over-salting may affect subsequent acid development. Without the inhibitive effect of acid the growth of undesirable pathogens could occur;
- under-salting may allow the growth of pathogens such as Staphylococcus aureus.

The **control measures** are:-

-           for our batch processing, the addition of a known quantity of salt and thorough mixing to ensure even distribution.

Unsalted curd will not be allowed to progress through the system.

4.1.11   Pressing and wrapping

The **hazards** to consider here are:-

-           cross-contamination from presses, equipment and, especially, moulds;
-           contamination of curd by food handlers in manual fill operations.

The **control measures** include:-

-           defined and scheduled cleaning procedures and effective mould washing;
-           appropriate training, facilities and work instructions to ensure hygienic handling.

4.1.12   Maturation

The **hazards** to consider here are:-

-           survival of pathogens during storage;
-           unwrapped cheese may be subjected to contamination by pests, especially cheese mites and other insects.

The **control measures** include:-

-           maturation time;
-           maturation temperature;
-           pest control, including proofing, trapping and routine inspections by qualified personnel/contractors.

4.1.13   Cutting and packing

The **hazards** to consider here are:-

-           cross-contamination from equipment and environment;
-           contamination of cheeses by food handlers;
-           ineffective vacuum packaging or gas flushing, allowing mould growth.

The **control measures** include:-

-        defined and scheduled cleaning procedures for both equipment and
         factory environment;

-        appropriate training, facilities and work instructions to ensure
         hygienic handling;

-        regular pack integrity monitoring.

4.1.14   Storage and distribution

The **hazard** to be considered here is:-

-        mould growth

The **control measures** include:-

-        temperature control/monitoring of cold store (optimum <5°C, 8°C
         max);

-        monitoring of shelf-life performance.

4.1.15   Overview of process

Throughout the process a major **hazard** is re-contamination from plant or
environment.

The following **control measures** are, therefore, recommended:-

-        raw milk storage is at opposite end of the room from pasteurised milk
         vat. Pasteurised equipment is given a separate C.I.P.;

-        cleaning is critical and effective cleaning regimes must be set up for
         all plant and equipment;

-        good hygienic practice covers handling practices throughout cheese
         manufacture and control of personnel involved;

-        it is essential to avoid cross-contamination from the environment.
         This is partly controlled by segregation as above, but must also
         include control of access from other factory area through a triple door
         system.

5. CCP Decision Tree

The CCps in this flow diagram were verified using the CODEX Decision Tree.

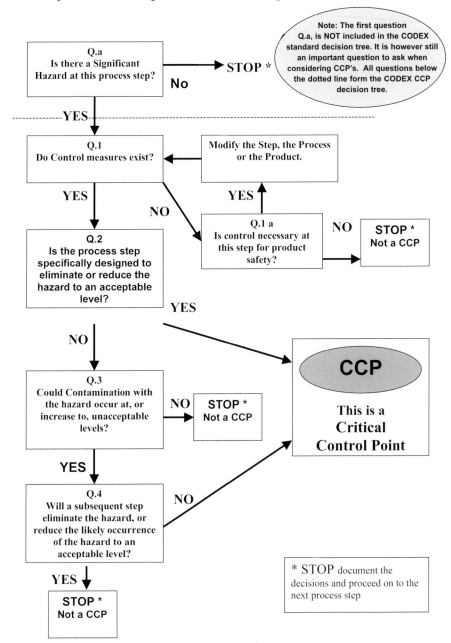

Note: The first question Q.a, is NOT included in the CODEX standard decision tree. It is however still an important question to ask when considering CCP's. All questions below the dotted line form the CODEX CCP decision tree.

Q.a
Is there a Significant Hazard at this process step?

STOP *

No

------------- YES --

Q.1
Do Control measures exist?

Modify the Step, the Process or the Product.

YES

NO

YES

Q.1 a
Is control necessary at this step for product safety?

NO

STOP *
Not a CCP

Q.2
Is the process step specifically designed to eliminate or reduce the hazard to an acceptable level?

YES

NO

Q.3
Could Contamination with the hazard occur at, or increase to, unacceptable levels?

NO

STOP *
Not a CCP

CCP

This is a **Critical Control Point**

YES

Q.4
Will a subsequent step eliminate the hazard, or reduce the likely occurrence of the hazard to an acceptable level?

NO

YES

STOP *
Not a CCP

* STOP document the decisions and proceed on to the next process step

6.   General Comment

In preparing a HACCP for artisanal cheesemaking all staff and the local Environmental Health Officer need to be involved for best results. Where farmers or cheesemakers have no previous experience of HACCP it is recommended that a suitably qualified consultant be employed to help through the process and also provide certificated HACCP training to a recognized standard, e.g. RIPH, SOFHT or EHO.

Although a HACCP is required by law, it is a fundamental tool in the quest for Safe Food Production and business protection. A HACCP should always be prepared for any food process before building the food process premises as this will ensure that suitable controls are built into the building, e.g. preventing cross-contamination by suitable segregation of areas. Best practice is to isolate raw milk storage from other milk handling areas.

7.   Pre-requisites for HACCP, sometimes referred to as PRP's

The pre-requisites are normally prepared before the HACCPs. They are as follows:

1. Good Manufacturing Practice (Hygiene)
2. Good Laboratory Practice
3. Calibration
4. Pest control
5. Incident and Recall Management Systems
6. Preventive Maintenance Programme
7. Training
8. Supplier Quality Assurance

7.1   Good Manufacturing Practice

This is covered in Policy Documents 1 and 2 and in Plant Cleaning and Hygiene Manual, which has been prepared by the detergent and sterilant suppliers. This manual also has the cleaning plans for all plant, equipment, floor, walls, light fittings and ceilings. A tick record sheet is also available for signing to confirm that planned cleaning has been carried out.

Waste will be removed daily from the dairy and disposed of to meet legislative and good practice.

Water is sourced from the mains supply and is suitably treated and tested as potable water on a regular basis. Monthly checks are carried out for Coliforms and e-coli. Annual checks are carried out on the chemical composition of the water.

All staff have to complete a Health Questionnaire on an annual basis, (see Attachment A), and a Return to Work Health Questionnaire if they have been sick, particularly after a foreign holiday, (see Attachment B).

Appropriate manufacturing records are completed daily, including the signing of the pasteuriser thermograph and the appropriate cheesemaking record, see Staffordshire Cheese and Camembert.

The EU identification mark is applied to retail pack labels and bulk cheese labels.

Product Identification and Traceability:

A. the cheesemaking record has identification details of each ingredient to allow traceability if required;

B. when cheese is packed after pressing it is given a label with the cheese name and date of manufacture;

C. when cheese is packaged for sale it has relevant product labels, e.g. Captain Smith's Titanic, plus a label giving the weight, date of manufacture, date of packing and best before date.

7.2 Good Laboratory Practice

Only laboratories who are nationally accredited are used for the milk, product and water testing.

Dairy product sampling rate is covered in Attachment C and microbiological criteria in Attachment D. Water testing requirements are covered in Attachment E.

7.3 Calibration

Retail scales are externally calibrated annually and checked daily for accuracy with a stamped 250gm weight.

The hand held digital thermometer is externally calibrated annually and checked weekly by plunging the probe into boiling water and ice. The results are recorded in the cheese day book.

The pasteuriser thermograph is calibrated annually and checked daily against the hand held digital thermometer. The thermograph is signed by the pasteuriser operator to confirm that this check has been carried out.

7.4   Pest Management Systems

External specialists are employed. Eight visits per annum are carried out. On each visit an audit report is completed and the specialist is attended by the cheesemaker who arranges any appropriate corrective action. A dairy drawing, with bait points identified, is available.

7.5   Incident and Recall Management

This is covered in the Recall Procedure (Attachment F).

An important "After the Event" Document is the Corrective and Preventive Action Form (see Attachment G), which is used to analyse and prevent future recalls. This same document is used to analyse internal quality problems, supplier and customer problems.

7.6   Preventive Maintenance

Company vehicles are subject to appropriate maintenance by external specialists.

The pasteuriser is checked on an annual basis by external engineers and appropriate records are available.

Refrigeration equipment and retail scales are also externally maintained.

7.7   Training

All staff are trained to certificate level in basic hygiene, certificate level in HACCP and given specific job training for all areas of the cheese manufacturing and packaging until they reach their individual level of competence. An individual Training Record (see Appendix 2) is completed for all staff. This also records when they are checked for competence following basic training. The staff are evaluated for effectiveness of training and are re-trained if necessary.

7.8   <u>Supplier Quality Assurance</u>

Milk is sourced from Dairy Farmers from Britain who conduct planned Quality Assurance of all farm milk supplies, including bacteriological and compositional control of the milk. Each milk delivery is accompanied by a computer generated volume and temperature record. These volumes and temperature recording are independently checked by us and the delivery note signed to confirm agreement. If there are any failures on milk volume, temperature, appearance or odour appropriate action is taken, including the completion of a Corrective and Preventive Action Form (Attachment G) is completed.

Monthly laboratory analysis are provided by Dairy Farmers from Britain for microbiological and chemical analysis.

Starters and other ingredients are only purchased from quality accredited companies. Currently we source starters and rennet from Chr. Hansen.

8.   Seven HACCP Principles

The Staffordshire Cheese Company HACCP follows the seven HACCP Principles:

1. Conduct a hazard analysis (identify any hazards that must be prevented or controlled)
2. Determine the critical control points (CCP's)
3. Establish critical limits, target levels and tolerances
4. Establish a monitoring system for CCP's
5. Establish corrective actions to be taken when a CCP is outside its limits
6. Establish verification procedures (to ensure that the HACCP is working effectively)
7. Establish documentation and records for HACCP

NOTE: A hazard is a biological, chemical or physical agent, in,. or a condition of, food with the potential to cause an adverse health effect – CODEX definition.

9.   Validating the HACCP

The Process Flow Diagram is checked each time a new cheese product is made to ensure that it continues to be an accurate representation of the process at all times.

A validation record is completed annually (see Attachment H) to ensure that the HACCP will continue to give safe food.

The verification of the HACCP process is completed on every cheesemaking day by ensuring that the pasteuriser thermograph accurately records pasteurizing temperature and that the operator signs to confirm this. The cheese process records are fully completed, especially the recording of acid test results which demonstrate whether the starter cultures are working correctly and producing safe food. If a 'slow' cheese is made, i.e. in the Staffordshire Cheese, if the correct acidities are not reached in 6 hours from renneting then the cheese will be rejected to an appropriate disposal source.

10.   Attachments to the HACCP

Policy No. 1	Personal Hygiene
Policy No. 2	Cleaning and Disinfection
A	Health Questionnaire
B	Return to Work Health Questionnaire
C	Dairy Product Sampling Rate
D	Microbiological Criteria
E	Water Testing
F	Recall Procedure
G	Corrective and Preventive Action Form
H	Annual Validation Record for HACCP

POLICY NO. 1

Our aim is to produce safe, high quality cheese employing trained staff committed to good personal hygiene standards and clean operating methods.

Personal Hygiene relates to:

Raw milk   - operating methods, milking and raw milk storage

Cheesemaking duties   - any aspect of cheese making, cheese handling or storage

The aim is to ensure that:

Animal disease is controlled   - good veterinary care, hygiene practices and clean conditions

Raw milk is protected   - adopt clean milking and milk handling practices

Cheese is not contaminated   - follow rules of good hygienic practice at all stages

Key Principles

- Pay particular attention to thorough hand washing, especially after visiting the toilet
- Report any symptoms of illness for a decision about your work duties
- Record any incidents where hygiene provisions need further attention
- Adopt hygienic working practices
- Seek advice if in doubt

Rules of good personal hygiene

- Wash hands when entering any production area and before handling milk or cheese
- Wash hands after visiting the toilet, eating/drinking or handling waste or dirty items
- Wear clean protective clothing and hair coverings
- Report illness such as food poisoning, gastric problems, coughs/colds
- Do not work with milk or cheese if in doubt about personal illness
- Cover cuts and sores with coloured, waterproof dressings. Further protect using rubber gloves.

- Ensure that finger nails are cut short and clean
- Refrain from unhygienic habits which could contaminate milk or cheese, such as:
  - coughing, sneezing over or near products
  - touching your mouth, nose, ears or hair whilst working
- Do not eat, drink or smoke in production areas
- Do not bring personal items into the production areas or wear jewellery
- Do not move between external areas and production areas without changing protective clothing, footwear and washing hands
- Forbid non-authorised persons from entering the production area
- Ensure that authorised visitors wear suitable protective clothing, and are not left unattended.

We undertake to ensure that:

- Adequate hygiene facilities are available to support this policy
- Personal hygiene and hygiene practice standards are maintained
- Staff are adequately instructed, supervised and trained to fulfill requirements

POLICY NO. 2   CLEANING AND DISINFECTION

Our aim is to prevent the contamination of milk or cheese from equipment, personnel or premises and by maintaining sanitary conditions, within and around the premises.

Cleaning and disinfection relates to:

Premises & surroundings	- removal of all potential sources of contamination
Equipment	- removal of soiling followed by chemical or thermal disinfection

The aim is to reduce:

Sources of contamination	- keep floors, walls, fittings, environment & surroundings clean
Bacterial survival	- use an approved means of disinfection of food contact surfaces
Other contamination	- take action to remove cleaning chemicals or foreign bodies

Key Principles

- Keep premises clean at all times. Clean as you go
- Rinse and wash equipment immediately after use
- Use correct chemicals, strength, temperature and contact time
- Protect equipment from contamination after cleaning

Rules of cleaning and disinfection   *Premises*

- Adopt a clean as you go policy. This means that:
    o Any soiling, debris or waste must be cleared away promptly
    o Floors must be regularly brushed and washed down
    o Drains must be kept clean and free from blockage
    o Soiling of walls or fittings must be cleaned promptly
    o At the end of each work period the interior must be left thoroughly clean
    o Keep all storage and ripening areas dry and swept clean
    o Ensure that waste disposal areas are kept tidy and brushed clean each day

o   Keep approaches swept clean and swilled down daily

Equipment

- Include any surface having contact with milk, ingredients or cheese
- Rinse with plain water immediately after use, to avoid dried residues
- Wash all equipment as soon as possible, using the correct cleaning chemicals
- Follow correct routines, ensuring that:
  o   Chemicals are used at the required strength
  o   Adequate water is used at the required temperature
  o   Sufficient chemical or heat contact time is allowed to ensure disinfection
  o   Equipment is adequately rinsed
- Position equipment after washing to allow natural drainage
- Protect equipment from contamination, e.g. dust or flying insects
- Inspect equipment before use for residues or scale and treat accordingly
- Keep all cleaning equipment and chemical containers clean and tidy

We undertake to ensure that:

- Adequate cleaning facilities and chemicals are available to support this policy
- Premises and equipment are kept in a suitable condition for adequate cleaning

Staff are adequately instructed, supervised and trained to fulfil requirements.

Attachment A

EMPLOYEE / VISITOR'S HEALTH SCREENING QUESTIONNAIRE

To be completed by all employees on an annual basis and external visitors wishing to enter The Staffordshire Cheese Company Ltd. production facility. Admission is at the discretion of the Owner.

NAME:

ORGANISATION:

DATE:

Have you recently suffered any sickness, diarrhea or stomach disorder over the last 3 months?	YES	NO
Have you been into contact with anyone with the above symptoms?	YES	NO
Have you any history of, or contact with Typhoid, Paratyphoid?	YES	NO
Have you visited any other food premises in the last 72 hours, if so which?	YES	NO
Have you any history of, or contact with Hepatitis or jaundice?	YES	NO
Have you any history of skin conditions, eczema, dermatitis?	YES	NO
Have you any history of disease of, or discharge from the nose, ears or eyes?	YES	NO
Have you recently been abroad, if so which country and for how long?	YES	NO
Have you been ill whilst abroad, or since your return to the UK?	YES	NO
Have you a history of oral hygiene diseases?	YES	NO
Have you any history of bronchitis or productive cough?	YES	NO
Have you any history or contact with tuberculosis?	YES	NO
Have you been on a farm recently?	YES	NO

Signature of employee or visitor: ....

Signature of director: ....

Attachment B

HEALTH QUESTIONNAIRE FOR EMPLOYEES WHO HAVE BEEN SICK OR HAVE TRAVELLED OVERESEAS

This form MUST be completed by all employees on return to work after ANY ILLNESS OR FOREIGN VISIT and returned to the owner to obtain agreement to commence work.

Name of Employee:

Have you been abroad: YES / NO

If YES, please state countries visited:

Since you have been away, have you suffered from sickness, diarrhea or any stomach disorder?	YES	NO
Have you had any 'flu like' symptoms in the last 48 hours?	YES	NO
Have you been in contact with anyone with Typhoid, Paratyphoid, Cholera, Dysentery, Salmonella infection, Gastro-enteritis, or any of the symptoms above?	YES	NO
Are you suffering from any infection of the skin, eyes, ears, nose, throat or gums?	YES	NO

If the answer to any of the questions is YES, you may not start work until you have contacted the Owner.

I acknowledge that failure to disclose information may require reassessment of my fitness and could lead to termination of my employment.

SIGNATURE OF EMPLOYEE: .... DATE:

CHECKED BY DIRECTOR: .... DATE:

Attachment C

DAIRY PRODUCTS (HYGIENE) REGULATIONS 1995 – RECOMMENDED SAMPLING FREQUENCIES FOR OPERATORS

PRODUCT (As specified in the Schedules)	TEST/ORGANISM	RECOMMENDED SAMPLING FREQUENCY
Schedule 3 **Part II** Raw cow's milk for the production of - HT drinking milk - Fermented milk - Junket - Jellied milk - Flavoured milk - Cream	Plate count at 30°C (per ml) Somatic cell count (per ml)	2 per month (min. required by paragraph 4 of Part II) 1 per month (min. required by paragraph 4 of Part II)
Raw cows' milk for the manufacture of any other dairy products	Plate count at 30°C (per ml)? Somatic cell count (per ml)?	2 per month (min. required by paragraph 4 of Part II) 1 per month (min. required by paragraph 4 of Part II)

[1] These tests do not apply to products covered by Regulation 9(12), nor, for the time being, to products which could be regarded as 'traditional' under Regulation 9(13)

Attachment D

PRODUCT (As specified in the Schedules)	TEST/ORGANISM	RESULTS REQUIRED	TEST PROCEDURE
Criteria for raw milk collected from production holding	Plate count at 30°C (per ml)[1]	≥ 100,000	Rolling average over 2 month period, at least 2 samples per month.
	Somatic cell count (per ml)[1]	≥ 400,000	Average over 3 months, at least 1 sample per month.
	Free from antibiotic residues	As stated in EC Reg 2377/90	Ongoing requirement.
Raw milk immediately before processing	Plate count at 30°C (per ml)[1]	< 300,000 per ml	If fails operator to inform LA, take measure to correct.
All dairy products able to support growth of Listeria monocytogenes. (intended specifically for infants higher standard)	Listeria monocytogenes	Absent in 25g	Before food has left producer
	Listeria monocytogenes	Less than 100 cfu/g	Products placed on market during shelf life.
			Immediate withdrawal of product required
Pasteurised milk and cream	Phosphatase test	Flouophos-less than 500 mU/1 advised less than 100mU/1 A-M test less than 4 ug/1	
Pasteurised milk and other pasteurised liquid dairy products	Enterobacteriaceae	2/5 m <1 cfu/ml M – 5 cfu/ml	At end of manufacturing process. Action-check on efficiency of heat treatment and prevention of contamination and raw milk quality
Cheese from pasteurised milk	E.Coli	2/5 m = 100 cfu/g M = 1,000 cfu/g	Improvements in production hygiene and selection of raw materials required.

Attachment E

MONTHLY BACTERIOLOGICAL TESTS ON WATER

E.Coli   Absent in 100ml

TVC   Evaluate over first three months

Coliforms   Absent in 100mls

Listeria Absent

ANNUAL CHEMICAL TESTS

Turbidity

Taste and odour

Conductivity

pH

Lead

Nitrates

Attachment F

RECALL PROCEDURE

A recall may be required following information from customers or independent agencies which indicate the possibility of a serious health risk.

A recall may also be actioned by the owner of Staffordshire Cheese Company where it is considered it necessary, e.g. serious product fault.

1.   Possible Problem Product

    1.1   Time and date of receipt of information:

    1.2   Date product received by customer:

    1.3   Name of person supplying information:

            Telephone Number:

    1.4   Product 'Use By' Code and description:

    1.5   Nature of problem (try to retrieve suspect sample):

    1.6   Where did it occur:

    1.7   When did it occur:

    1.8   Number of individuals affected:

    1.9   Health Authority involved:

            Contact Name: Tel. No.

2.   Recall Action

    2.1   Check that suspect product was manufactured by R J Eyres & Sons:
            Who: OWNER or designate   YES ☐ NO ☐

    2.2   Check 'Use By' Code and what customers have received and in what quantity:
            Who: OWNER or designate

    2.3   Check production before and after suspect production date to decide if additional product needs to be recalled or quarantined if still in stock.
            Who: OWNER or designate

    2.4   Check invoices and deliveries for Use By Codes and arrange to recall all suspect product.
            Who: OWNER or designate

    2.5   Check Packing Record: YES ☐ NO ☐

    2.5   Check Daily Sales Sheet for Customers and attach copy.

Attachment F

RECALL CHECK SHEET

DATE:

Customer Name	Contact Name	Tel. No.	Fax No.	E-mail	Date Product received by customer	Product type & quantity supplied	Product type and quantity to be returned	Customer contacted YES	NO

NOTES:

NB 1: If there is a discrepancy between the product supplied and the product to be returned appropriate action will be taken by the OWNER in consultation with the customer and local authority.

NB 2: Only the owner or designate should deal with the customers, external agencies and the press.

Attachment G

CORRECTIVE / PREVENTIVE ACTION REPORT

Customer Complaint ☐	Supplier Complaint ☐	Non-conforming Product ☐	Internal Problem ☐

CORRECTIVE/PREVENTIVE ACTION REPORT NUMBER:

PROBLEM:

SIGNATURE	**DATE**

WHAT WENT WRONG?

SIGNATURE	**DATE:**

CORRECTIVE / PREVENTIVE ACTION TO BE TAKEN:	Proposed completion date	Actual completion date
SIGNATURE	DATE:	

Review Date:	
Date of Action Completion:	
Reviewed by (Title)	
Signed:	Date:
The Problem has been successfully eliminated	

Attachment H

HACCP VALIDATION CHECK RECORD

HACCP Plan Validation Section	YES	NO
Is the scope an accurate description of the process?		
Are there accurate validated flow charts identifying each step in the process?		
Are all significant hazards correctly identified and addressed?		
Are appropriate control measures in place for all stages of the process?		
Are all CCPs justified? (Record of Y/N decision process)		
Are critical limits acceptable?		
Are there appropriate procedures for monitoring at CCP's?		
Are corrective actions documented, in place and understood by relevant staff?		
Is there adequate documentation and records to support the HACCP Plan and all activities in practice?		
SUMMARY Are all relevant hazards addressed?		
Does the plan control all hazards if followed correctly?		
VALIDATION RECORD Validation Carried Out By:*		
Position:		
Signed:	Date of Validation:	

VALIDATION CHECKS: This is to confirm that all relevant hazards are being addressed and that the Plan would control all relevant hazards if it is followed correctly.

A validation check should be carried out before the plan is first implemented to make sure it is thorough and accurate. If the Plan is in any way incomplete or inaccurate it must be amended.

*The HACCP Team or an external expert may carry out validations.
Validation checks should also be carried out whenever the Plan is reviewed.

Appendices

Appendix 1

Application to register the Staffordshire Cheese as a Product of Designated Origin (PDO)

1. **Competent Authority**
   Department for the Environment, Food and Rural Affairs
   Food Chain, Marketing and Competitiveness Division
   Regional and Local Foods Branch, Room 338, Nobel House
   17 Smith Square, London, SWIP 3JR United Kingdom

2. **Applicant**
   Mr J Knox, Staffordshire Cheese Company, Glenmore House, 55 Rose Bank
   Leek, Staffordshire, ST13 6AG

3. **Name of Product**
   The Staffordshire Cheese

4. **Type of Product**
   cheese – class 1.3

5. a) Name: The Staffordshire Cheese

   b) **Description of Product**
   The Staffordshire Cheese is made from milk from cows kept on Staffordshire farms. It has a smooth, slightly crumbly texture which can be hard or semi-hard depending on the age of maturity (2-12 months and 2-4 weeks respectively), a pale cream colour and is creamy, fresh and lactic in flavour. The cheese is cylindrical in shape, weighs 8-10 kgs, measures 10 and a quarter inches and is sold cloth-bound. (see photos at annex 1)

   c) **Definition of Geographical Area**
   The County of Staffordshire in England (see maps attached at annex 2, covering the County and the location of the County within the UK).

d)   **Proof of Origin**

Cistercian monks settled in Leek, Staffordshire in the 13th century. The monks
came from Poulton Abbey on the Banks of the River Dee, Cheshire. In April
1214 a small group of Cistercian Monks, led by their Abbot, Richard of
Poulton, arrived at the outskirts of the Manor of Leek in North Staffordshire.
Before the Norman Conquest, the manor was held by Algarus Coi; in the reign
of King Stephen by Ranulph, Earl of Chester, who gave the tithes of his mill
here to the monks of St. Werberge, at Chester. His grandson, the sixth Earl of
Chester, gave his manor to the monks of the Abbey of Dieu le Cryse or Dieu
Encres, which he founded in Leek Frith, in the valley of the Churnet, about 2
miles north of the town of Leek.

The Cistercian Monks led a life of prayer, study and work. The monks set
out to be self sufficient and were agriculturalists, potters, bakers, brewers,
cheesemakers and printers. In Leek and the surrounding area the monks were
famous for their flocks of sheep. In the booklet 'A Cistercian Monk's Life
Yesterday and Today' by Gillian Ellis, printed by Cistercian Monks, Mount
Saint Bernard Abbey, Coalville, Leicester, it is recorded that "they had only
one main meal a day, taken about noon. There were two courses first vegetable
soup or thick porridge, then bread, fruit, and some cheese".

The monks brought their cheesemaking skills with them to Leek. At the
dissolution of the Dieulacres Monastery in the 16th Century two wooden
cheese vats and a cheese brining tank were recorded in their list of assets. This
has been confirmed by the Rev. Michael J. Fisher MA who wrote the book
Dieulacres Abbey. (see annex 3)

Cheese fairs were established in Staffordshire in 1597 and were held
monthly, reducing to 3 times a year, on the second Monday in March, and the
third Mondays in September and November, by 1821. (See annex 4 'White's
Dictionary of Staffordshire')

In the 19th century, records show local cheese factors and factories. (See
annex 5 "Alstonfield a Village History, chapter 'The Old Cheese Factory at
Hopedale') ....'The cheese manufactory was registered and opened in 1874 by
20 farmers and was a move towards co operative farming. The whey was
settled and put into a tank which still exists. On top was a bucket pump where
people came to collect whey to feed their pigs. The cheese was made at the
north end of the factory and the stone rennet shelves still exists in the kitchen.

The second room downstairs contained racks where the cheeses were turned
while maturing'. Annex 6: 'The Victorian History of Stafford Vol. VII' tells of
the cheesemakers in Staffordshire in the 19th and early 20th century,

delivery note, which links back to the dairy farm and forward to the final pressed cheese in the maturing room. Page 6 of the Food Standard Agency's Food Safety Workbook contains brief details of the above.

Traceability of the cheese at point of sale

Page 43 of the Food Standards Agency's Food Safety Workbook is a documented record of the food safety management system. As well as covering the quality assurances given by the suppliers of raw ingredients used in making the cheese it also covers the traceability of the cheese once it leaves the production site. If the cheese is sold whole, the manufacturing date is on the invoice, if it is sold in portions it has on the label the packing date, which links back to the processing record for the manufacturing details. This is covered by the maintenance of batch and stock records, sales invoices and details of customers.

Food Standards Agency's Food Safety Workbook is at annex 10.

e)   **Method of Production**

Fresh raw milk from farms within the county of Staffordshire (see annex 9 for letter of confirmation of this from the Dairy Farmers of Britain) is held overnight at a chilled temperature of 0-5°C . On day two, Staffordshire cream (also sourced from farms within the county) is added to the milk and stirred in for 15 minutes. This milk/ cream mixture is pasteurised at 72-75.5°C for 15-20 seconds. The mixture is then pumped into a cheese vat and a temperature of 32.5- 35°C achieved. At 28°C 0.2-0.4% mixed starter cultures are added to the milk for acid development and flavour.

After 60 to 75 minutes of ripening at 32.5°C, rennet is added at the temperature of 31-33°C. The rennet coagulation takes 45-50 minutes and is tested by hand before cutting.

Curd will then be firm with a clean break. After 35-45 minutes the curd is then cut the length of the vat and across the vat with a vertical knife, and then cut with a horizontal knife in the same manner. This takes 20 minutes.

The curds are then stirred at 30-32°C for 40 minutes. They are then settled and the whey is drawn through a sieve at the end of the vat for 35 minutes. At the completion of the whey-off, the acidity will be 0.29% lactic whey. The curds are then broken every 15 minutes over a period of 45 minutes. Acidity at first break is 0.39%, at second break 0.45% and at the final break 0.53% lactic acid.

including Samuel Mellor, Bartholomew Massey, Anthony Massey, William Shirley and his son Samuel Shirley who was the first secretary of the Manifold Valley Dairies Ltd, which had a cheese factory in the county.

This Staffordshire Cheese continued to be produced until the advent of the Second World War, when the central milk gathering policy by the Milk Marketing Board spelt the end of many English regional cheeses. Until then, many farms in the county produced the cheese. This application therefore represents the revival (by an artisan cheesemaker co-operating with local farmers) of this traditional cheese lost, as so many were, to wartime food supply policy.

The revived cheese is establishing its reputation amongst retailers and consumers. It has won an award at Bakewell Show cheese competition (copy of award attached at annex 7) and is being sold at delicatessens, farmers' markets, farm shops, garden centres, restaurants, pubs, and by mail order. The Staffordshire Tourist Board is also very supportive of this revived county cheese and would like to see it helped by a PDO to gain a place in the culinary tourist experience.

(See annex 8: press cutting evidence of cheese history and revival and evidence of increasing reputation of the cheese, including a photo of the producer showing his cheese under his Regional Food Group banner (Heart of England Fine Foods) at a food fair).

The milk and cream used for the cheese are, as previously mentioned, sourced entirely from 6 or 7 farms within the county of Staffordshire. At annex 9 is a letter of confirmation concerning the provenance of the milk and cream from the organisation 'Dairy Farmers of Britain' ((DFB) a large dairy farmers' co-operative through which the milk for the Staffordshire cheese is bought).

Traceability of the milk and cream

DFB milk tankers each have a specific collection route and on-board computers which note the farm details, milk volume, milk temperature and date of collection. When the DFB tanker delivers to the Staffordshire Cheese Company, the on-board computer generates a delivery note giving milk volume, tanker route number, milk temperature and delivery date. The DFB has a central computer system called 'Core Milk System' into which all milk tankers download information daily, including tanker route, farm collection point and chemical and bacterial analysis of milk collected. The Staffordshire Cheese Company's dairy has a cheese process record compiled from the DFB

The curds are then broken by stainless steel peg mill. 2.5% salt is added to the curds during milling. The salt is mixed in by turning the curds with a food-grade plastic shovel once and by hand three times. The cheese is only turned 4 times in total as any more would dry out the curds.

Then the salted cheese curds are hand filled to muslin cloth-lined stainless steel moulds. The cloths have sewn in circular bases, and the moulds are specially made for whey drainage and cheese shape. The cheeses are then pressed at 2lbs per square inch at 21-25°C overnight. After pressing, the cheese cloth is smoothly covering the surface of the cheese. The cheeses are stored on shelves at 7-10°C, turned daily for one week and weekly thereafter. The mild cheese is ripe in 2-4 weeks, but can be matured for up to 12 months.

Full details of the manufacturing process, traceability and confirmation that at all times, production standards are observed in accordance with the Food Standards Agency's guidelines are contained within the Food Standards Agencies Food Safety Workbook at annex 10 and in the above paragraph detailing the proof or origin.

(see also annex 11: photos and description of parts of the cheesemaking process).

f)   **Link to the Geographical Area**
The county of Staffordshire has a warm, wet, westerly climate and a carboniferous limestone terrain, producing lush grazing pasture which produces the creamy milk that gives the cheese its character. An extract from the book 'The General View of Agriculture of the County of Stafford ` by W Pitt of Penderford (see annex 12) quotes him as saying "The quantity of limestone in the Moorlands area is inexhaustible, being in many places in the strata of immense thickness. This is the best part of the Moorlands and the soil seems to have a natural aptitude for producing a fine herbage of grass". The properties of this grass are essential to the nature of the Staffordshire cheese. All milk and cream used to make the Staffordshire cheese are produced from this pasture (see earlier annex 9).

In addition, this cheese is characterised by history and tradition in its link to the area. (See annex 13 'Staffordshire and Warwickshire' by John Alfred Longford, chapter `The Agriculture of Staffordshire) ` ....the county consists chiefly of cheesemaking districts, where pasturage prevails ...The reasons for this are simple. The soil of Staffordshire being much more suited to the production of grass than of wheat or other corn, dairy farming is more profitable than arable cultivation ...' '...during the winter months   from

November to early May milking cows are tied up in the sheds, whereby half the litter required in open yards is saved. The calving time is usually early April, the period most desirable on cheese farms because the cows are then in full profit at the best time of year, when the best cheese is made ....cheese making is sometimes continued through out the year ...a first rate cow will yield throughout the year £14 worth of cheese...'.

The 'proof of origin' section details the cheesemaking traditions and the factories, fairs etc where the cheese was made and sold. Also, the revival of the reputation of the cheese and its increasing sales. It is worth noting that the current producer has decided not to trade with large supermarkets yet, preferring to re- establish the cheese in outlets such as farmers' markets, farm shops, local delicatessens and by mail order.

g)   **Inspection body**
Staffordshire County Council Trading Standards Service
24 Horninglow Street, Burton-on -Trent, Staffordshire DE14 1PG

The inspection body is an official public body conforming to the principles of the EN 45011 standard.

h)   **Labelling**
Approved symbol will be used at point of sale, or on any packaging containing the product. An example of the current label used on the cheese is at annex 14.

Appendix 2

CHEESE TRAINING RECORD

NAME:

	BASIC	KNOWLEDGE	COMPETENT
Milk Tests			
Milk Pasteurisation			
Cleaning Pasteuriser			
Prepare Starter			
Add starter to vat			
Measure and add rennet			
Test Coagulum			
Cut coagulum			
Stir vat			
Run whey			
'Cheddar'			
Test whey			
Complete cheese record			
Salt preparation			
Mill and salt			
Fill Staffordshire Mould			
Fill Archie's Choice mould			
Make cheese and chives			
Wax cheese			
Cut cheese for market			
Label price/weight for market			
Fill chill boxes for market			
Fill green box for market			

Appendix 3
Cheese process records

VARIETY: Staffordshire	Milk Volume:	litres	Cream Volume:	litres
INCOMING MILK TEMP:	APPEARANCE:		SMELL:	
MILK TEMP. IN TANK (DAY 2) °C		% L.A.		
HEAT TREATMENT	74°C / 15 seconds			
Internal Cold Store:	External Cold Store:		Cheese Room Temp:	

Acidifying Culture		
Acidifying Culture addition		
Flavour Culture		
Other ☐		
% L.A. AT RENNETING Ripening Temperature / Time	32.5°C / 1h15	
Annatto addition	-	
Calcium addition	-	

Coagulant addition	20 mls single strength / 100 litres milk	

	Time from coagulant addition		Time from coagulant addition	
Cut	0h40			
Cut size	10 min. cut	15 mm		
Steam – on	0h50			
Scald		33°C		
		% LA		
Pitch Start	1h10			
Pitch Complete	1h50			
Whey off	2h05	0.29		
After Break 1 ☐	2h20	0.39		
After Break 3	2h35	0.45		
Salting ♣	2h50	0.53		

Salt Addition	2.3% w/v	
Press Room Temperature		
Pressure used and stages		

Maturing ♥	10°C max	

NOTES

☐ First break into 150mm lumps and then beak every 7 minutes gradually getting smaller until they are 60mm at salting.

♣ Spread 30% of salt onto curd and add remainder when curd put through peg mill

♥ Higher maturing temp. required to allow lipase to develop flavour. Higher temps than 10°C are risky.

NUMBER OF CHEESE		WEIGHT OF CHEESE	

CAMEMBERT	PROJECT:		ACTUAL	
INCOMING MILK TEMP:	APPEARANCE:		SMELL:	
TIME FROM MILKING		% L.A.	Room Temp. am	
			pm	
HEAT TREATMENT	65°C / 30 mins			
Internal Cold Store:				

Acidifying Culture	Flora Danica	
Other	P. Candidium	
% L.A. AT RENNETING Ripening Temperature / Time	0.18 - 0.2% LA 32°C/1hr 15mins	
Coagulant addition	20 - 30 mls single strength / 100 litres milk	

		Time from coagulant addition	Time from coagulant addition	
Cut	1 – 2.5hrs			
Cut size	30mm cubes			
Curd handling	Settle for 15 mins	Remove surface whey		
Mould filling	Transfer to open ended moulds	Stand on draining mats in stacking trays		
Drainage	Over 18 hrs turning every 5 hrs	Room temp. reduced from 28 to 18°C, 90 – 95% relative humidity		
Salting	Dry salted (6-9gms of salt/cheese) or brined in 26% salt bath for 1-1.5hrs at 12-14°C	Possibly dipped or sprayed with P.Candidum		
Storage	12 – 15°C	90 to 95% RH for 1 to 2 weeks. Turned regularly		
Packing	When well coated with mould	Pack in laminated or waxed paper. Store at 4°C		

NOTES

NUMBER OF CHEESE		WEIGHT OF CHEESE	

Appendix 4

Marketing assistance with cheese development

British Cheese Awards	01608 659325
British Cheese Board	0117 921 1744
Business Link	01543 460007
Dairy UK	020 7486 7244
DEFRA	020 7270 8780
Farm Retail Association	023 8036 2150
Food from Britain	020 7233 5111
John Knox Ltd	01538 399733
Milk Development Council	01285 646500
National Dairy Council	020 7499 7822
National Farmers' Union	020 7311 7200
Society of Dairy Technology	01768 354034
Specialist Cheesemakers' Association	020 725 32114
The Rural Hub	01785 278581
The Soil Association	0117 914 2407

Appendix 5

Suppliers

Cheese equipment

1	Cold Rooms	
	Mono Food Plant	07970 255138
2	Cheese vats	
	AFM Food Machinery	01963 33211
3	Cheese vats	
	Wincanton Engineering	01935 818800
4	Soft cheese equipment	01773 819198
5	Paul Moody plc	01777 701141
6	Cold rooms	
	RJB Refrigeration	01743 350682
7	Cold rooms	
	JC Refrigeration	01743 361187
8	SS Cheese moulds and knives	
	John Knox Ltd	01538 399733

Floors

Flowcrete HF	01889 584826
Flowdek Ltd	01902 380334
Floortex EP	0800 980 0852

Vacuum packers and wax tanks

Flute Machinery	01743 352956

Consultants

John Knox MSc, CSci, FCMI, MCQI, FIFST　　01538 399733

Development of cheese, yogurt and ice-cream production businesses and training.

HACCP Development, HACCP Training Centre, Business Plans.

Chris Ashby – AB Cheesemaking　　01949 842867

Cheesemaking courses and fermented milk product consultancy

Cheese finishes

Plasticoat – Stratton Sales	01749 838690
Cheese cloths – Stratton Sales	01749 838690
Cheese Cloths – Stewart Textiles	0161 788 2100
Wax – Stratton Sales	01749 838690
Coatings / waxes – DSM Food Ingredients	01827 250556
Smoking of cheese – Port of Lancaster Smokehouse	01524 751493

Detergents

CIP, Dairy Hygiene, Safety Training, Cleaning Schedules

o	Maurice Walton	01768 354034
o	Cameron Court	01925 234696
o	James Dodd	01538 361265

Cultures and rennet

Stratton Sales – Chr. Hansen agents	01749 838690
Danisco	01933 445548
Chr. Hansen	01635 38343

Protective clothing, cheese cutters, brushes, hygiene equipment & laboratory equipment

Stratton Sales	01749 838690

Salt

The Salt Company	01270 611112

Cheese bags

Walshaw	0161 7972222

Pasteuriser maintenance and calibration

Dairy Engineers	01507 466987
Dairy Engineers	01422 823378

Appendix 6

Daily pastueriser detergent wash cycle procedure

1. MAKE SURE TO GET HOSE PIPE READY TO PUT WATER INTO RAW MILK TANK.

2. WAIT TILL YOU SEE WATER IN GLASS TUBE. TAKE OFF FLOAT VALVE INSIDE BALANCE TANK

3. TURN CHEESE VAT VALVE RIGHT – WATER NOW GOING DOWN DRAIN.

4. TURN RED VALVE NO. 2 BY 90° TO DRAIN BALANCE TANK. TURN BACK ON WHEN JUST ABOVE OUTLET HOLE. RINSE WITH WATER, LET OUT BY TURNING RED VALVE AGAIN - WHEN NEARLY EMPTY TURN VALVE AGAIN.

5. PUT ALL HEATERS ON ⑤ 60   DIVERSION ON 1

6. WATCH GLASS TUBE TILL WATER RUNS CLEAR. WASHING TEMPERATURE 85°c TURN VALVE 1 TO GO INTO BALANCE TANK.

7. TAKE OFF PIPE THAT GOES TO CHEESE MILK VAT TO ENSURE NO CONTAMINATION OF MILK. PUT IN BALANCE TANK.

8. TURN LAST TWO HEATERS OFF WHEN AT TEMPERATURE.

9. TOP VALVE TO LEFT (VALVE 1)

10. SHUT RED VALVE (TURN TO LEFT)

11. UNSCREW PIPE 2 FROM 4

12. NOW TURN VALVE 1 TO RIGHT

13. ADD DETERGENT $3\frac{1}{2}$ CUPS (NEED TO BUY CONTAINER FOR ADDING DETERGENT)

14. LEAVE RUNNING $\frac{1}{2}$ HOUR (LET AIR OUT)

15. HEATER 1 IS CONTROL HEATER. IF TEMPERATURE GETS TOO HOT TURN OFF HEATER 1 OR 2.

NOTE: WHEN WARMING UP AND COOLING DOWN DIVERSION SHOULD BE ON 1 WHEN AT TEMPERATURE TURN TO 2.

Pastueriser daily water rinsing after detergent washing procedure

1. SWITCH OFF HEATER

2. HOT WATER PUMP OFF

3. VALVE 1 TURN TO FACE BALANCE TANK ANTI-CLOCKWISE – GET GLOVES

4. CONNECT PIPE 2 TO PIPE 4

5. HOSE PIPE INTO BALANCE TANK

6. VALVE 1 BACK

7. TURN OFF WATER HOSE, WAIT TILL ? INCH FROM BOTTOM – SHOUT TO TURN WATER BACK ON SO ALL DETERGENT IS CLEANED OUT.

8. TAKE OFF PIPE COVER INSIDE AND CLEAN WHEN DIVERT COMES ON, LEAVE FOR 1 MINUTE.

9. LET TEMPERATURE ON RIGHT HAND GO TO 40°C TURN DIVERSION TO NO. 1.

10. LET BALANCE TANK DRAIN TO 2 INCHES READY FOR NEXT START UP.

11. TOP VALVE SWITCH OFF MILK PUMP DIVERSION SWITCH TO ZERO.

12. STICK BRUSH DOWN END OF PIPE (BY CHEESE VAT VALVE) WHEN CHEESE VAT IS EMPTY.

13. DON'T SPRAY WATER ON MACHINE – USE DAMP CLOTH

Daily cheese vat cleaning procedure

The cheese vat is cleaned daily when used.

CLEANING PRODUCT: Klenzray, Hypoklenz

TOOLS REQUIRED: Blue nylon bristled brush, hose pipe and
                                     stainless steel bucket

METHOD OF CLEANING:

When production is complete:

1. Using the hose, flush out any remaining curd

2. Make up a 2% solution of Klenzray in a bucket (200gms to 10 litres of water)

3. Using the brush with the solution, brush all surfaces of the vat, scrubbing to
   remove any stubborn deposits

4. Rinse with hose to remove all detergent traces

5. Make up a 200ppm solution of Hypoklenz in the garden spray

6. Spray all surfaces of the vat

7. Rinse before production is commenced.

Appendix 7

Tests on Starters: Vitality Test

One of the main points of this test is that it approaches very nearly actual cheesemaking conditions. The test is of special value in comparing a number of starters on any one day. Comparisons between starters tested on different days are much more uncertain.

Equipment

As many pint bottles as there are starters to be tested.

Water-bath or incubator thermostatically controlled at 30°C and 37°C.

Sterile pipettes – 1ml. and 10ml.

Measuring cylincer

Acidimeter

Method

1 Flash pasteurise a quantity of milk to 65.5°C (145 – 150°F)

2 Cool the milk to 30°C and measure 300ml. into each bottle

3 Add 3ml of starter, shake to mix and place in the 30°C incubator for 30 mins

4 Add 1ml. or rennet, mix by shaking for 3 – 5 secs. and replace in the 30°C incubator for 1 hour

5 Cut the curd into cubes and transfer the bottle to the incubator set at 37°C for 2 hours

6 Test whey for acidity, drain whey off and replace in the incubator for 1 hour

7 Repeat Step 6 and make final acidity test after a further hour's incubation

Summary

Time	Steps to be taken
0.00	Add 1% starter and incubate at 30°C
0.30	Add 1ml. of rennet and mix
1.30	Cut curd and incubate at 37°C
3.30	Take acidity, drain, and incubate at 37°C
4.30	Take acidity, drain, and incubate at 37°C
5.30	Take final acidity

The highest final acidity indicates the most active starters. Such starters show the greatest increase in acidity between the $4^1/_2$ and $5^1/_2$ hour reading

8 Record results

Appendix 8

The Lewis Method (ref. Cheese Vol1 JG Davis 1965)

United Dairies was prominent in devising a foolproof method for bulk starter propagation in the UK. Their work culminated in what is now known as the Lewis Method (1956).

The principle is that the starter milk and starter are at all times, during operations and culture, protected by a barrier of hypochlorite solution. It is physically impossible for any phage particle to gain access except through this solution, of course, kills it virtually instantaneously. No stopper or cover is removed from any culture or vessel at any time, and inoculations are made and samples withdrawn without breaking the seal.

This method is based on the use of vessels which are not only sealed by, but are completely immersed in water. The whole container is sealed in this way during the heating and the cooling of the milk, and even the inoculation of the culture, its growth and the propagation of the mother cultures are carried out while the whole of the container is protected in this way. No batch of starter is exposed to the atmosphere until the container is opened in teh cheese room.

Equipment

The only aperture leading in the container is 12mm in diameter into which is fitted a special rubber seal, e.g. of the Astell type. These seals adapt themselves to afford complete protection against the smallest particle from the atmosphere whether air is beign forced out of, or is being drawn into, the vessel.

The mother culture containers are made of polythene and may be sterilised by boiling or steaming. Any convenient size may be used for the bulk starter, but for most creameries a 45 litre can is suitable. If quantities greater than 900 litres are required it may be more convenient to use larger containers, but the method of use is identical for both portable cans and larger fixed vats or tanks.

When ready for transfer the culture is transferred using a double-ended hypodermic needle, the polythene bottles themselves being used to produce the pressure required. In order to give better control, the needles are fitted with plug-cocks. The needles are of a sufficient size to allow passage of the clotted starter at a reasonable speed. Larger diameter needles are used for the bulk starter inoculations.

The rubber seals are preferably made of rather softer rubber than those used in ordinary laboratory work. To prevent confusion the starter seals are conveniently made in a different colour. Although they last a very long time, it is a wise precaution to discard them after about two months'continuous use.

Heat treatment of the milk

Pure cultures should always be maintained in autoclaved milk, or somew other medium which has been efficiently sterilised. In the cheese industry, starter cultures are often maintained in milk heated to 90°C for 1 hour, and bulk starter may be grown in milk which has been held at 90°C for only 30 min.

This heat treatment is sufficient to kill phage and all vegetative bacterial cells, but starters which have become acclimatised to milk heated in this way may not show adequate activity in milk which has been more lightly heated. Lewis (1956) reported that starters grown in milk heated to 63 – 65°C for 45min. gave higher activities in the cheese vat than those maintained in autoclaved milk. It was also found that most phages were killed when the milk was heated to 63°C for 30 min., but one resisted a temperature of 66°C for the same time. The heat treatment for routine use was therefore raised to 70 – 73°C for 45 min.

Mother cultures

These are maintained in 4 oz (113.4 gms) narrow-necked polythene bottles. After washing in detergent they are sterilised over steam jet and filled with 0.1% hypochlorite solution. The seals are autoclaved and then held in hypochlorite. The mother culture is prepared by tipping out the hypochlorite and fillin in 3oz (85 gms)of bulk raw milk. The milk is then pasteurised at 70 – 73°C for 45 min. and thereafter held completely submerged in the cooling water, the whole being stored in a refrigerator until used.

This milk is inoculated by injecting a few drops of the desired culture by means of a hypodermic needle which pierces the special seals. Two needles, back to back, are used for this purpose, a plug-cock being fitted between them to give better control of the flow of starter. Any number of these may be prepared by autoclaving and storage in the hypochlorite solution.

Immediately before the inoculation the hollow place in the seal is filled with hypochlorite solutions and the needle assembly removed from the hypochlorite bath and one of the needles inserted through the solution and through the seal. The other needle is now pushed through the seal on the bottle of sterile milk, observing the same precautions. The cock is opened and the desired amount of starter squeezed from one bottle into the sterile milk. The cock is then turned off and the needle withdrawn.

The same technique may be used to obtain sample of the ripened starter for testing.

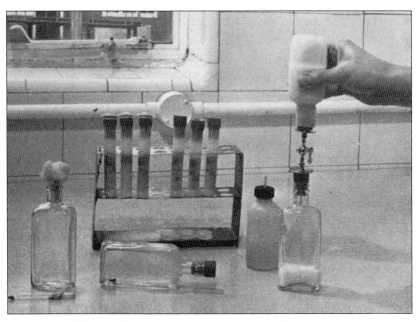

Inoculation of litmus milk plus chalk for maintenance of starter cultures.

(Astell Laboratory Services Co. Ltd.)

Washing and sterilising the polythene bottles to be used for starter.

(Astell Laboratory Services Co. Ltd.)

Working cultures

To avoid having to make a number of working cultures for a series of cans, a few large bottles can be used to inoculate the whole series. These are essentially the same as the small mother culture bottle, but hold about ³/₄ litre. The method of cleaning, sterilising, filling and inoculating is identical with that used for the mother cultures. Samples may be withdrawn from these for testing in exactly the same way. One such working culture can be used to inoculated 10 – 15 45 litre cans for bulk starter preparation.

Bulk starter

Irrespective of size or shape, all vessels must be constructed so that they can be completely closed after the initial stage of filling them with milk. There must be no vents or filters and all joints must be waterright. A small hole at the top of the vessel is closed in exactly the same way, using the same rubber seal as with the mother and working cultures. For the 45 litre can, a special lid is fabricated which can be screwed tightly against a rubber gasket. For large creameries, a 180 litre vessel is a convenient size.

The containers are steam-sterilised and then filled with bulk raw milk, but leaving a small air-space, e.g. putting 45 litres into the 45 litre can. The lids are fitted securely, the small hole fitted with a seal, and the vessels immersed in cold water. This water is heated by steam and the milk pasteurised at 70 – 73°C for a period of 45 min. The cans are then cooled to the incubation temperature of circa 22°C, which results in a slight positive pressure inside the cans. The vessels remain submerged throught the whole of the operation.

The bulk starter is inoculated in the same manner used for the mother cultures, but using needles of a large bore. from 50 to 100 ml. of starter is transferred from th working culture bottle to each 45 litre can if milk. After inoculations the milk is agitated in order to mix the starter thoroughly into the milk. This is conveniently done by rotating the vessel.

Appendix 9

John Knox Ltd
Business Development & Food Technology
Consultants

Skills Profile . . .

- Business development and Director level mentoring

- The development of Quality Management Systems for business improvement

- Advanced quality management - establishing quality management systems across a range of industries and company sizes, business audits, ISO 9000, BRC, EFSIS

- Profit Improvement through innovative reduction in wastage

- Dairy Food Technology, particularly cheese, yogurt, ice cream and milks

- Food Product Innovation and Food Business Development

- Training in Quality Systems Auditing and HACCP

- Information Technology Training

- Management teamwork development for business, people and innovation improvement

- Development of Five Year Business Plans

- Gaining grants for SMEs

- Training and Development of staff at all levels

- Chairman of the Members Relations Group of the Institute of Food Science and Technology for 7 years

- Chairman of the UK Processed Cheese Industry for 8 years

- Board Member of ASSIFONTE the European Industry Body

- Winner of the BBC Television Industrial Society Award for profit improvement through teamwork and innovative suggestion schemes

- Business Planning, Organisational development, Business appraisals, Strategic planning

- Investors in People - diagnosis and implementation

- Advanced management development and mentoring

John Knox Ltd
Business Development & Food Technology
Consultants

Services

John Knox MSc, C.Sci, FCMI, MCQI, FIFST is a qualified Business Development and Food Technology Consultant with over 35 years experience. He specialises in the Food Industry and has assissted small to medium sized companies and also larger organisations up to £1 billion turnover

Below is a list of the main services we offer:

- Working with SMEs to develop sound business plans and sales/marketing to achieve business growth

- Training individuals in Quality System Auditing across all business types

- Preparing companies for EFSIS, BRC and ISO9001 certification

- Training individuals to HACCP Certificate level for safe food production

- Working as part of management team to improve business profitability, including waste reduction

- Gaining grants for SMEs

- Development SME food businesses from concept to production start-up and product sales

- On-going innovation support in safe food production and product range improvement

- Special services to farmers and food companies in developing added value cheese, yogurt, ice cream, milks and fruit juices

- Dairy food engineering, food plant sourcing and installation for cheese, yogurt, ice-cream, milks and fruit juices

- John Knox has a range of specialists in chemistry, bacteriology, engineering and business management. These specialists work with John on projects covering food product development, factory design and installation and strategic developments for large businesses

Appendix 10

s p e c i a l i s t
CHEESE
MAKERS
a s s o c i a t i o n

this is to confirm that

The Staffordshire Cheese Company Ltd.

is a full Member of The Specialist Cheesmaker's Association

an organisation whose objectives are:

To promote awareness and appreciation of specialist cheeses among the public and trade.

To provide a forum in which Members can exchange views and ideas of mutual interest.

To present a unified voice to government, the EEC, the media and other parties.

To encourage excellence in cheesemaking.

Chairman

Date 15 February 1999

Certificate No. 334

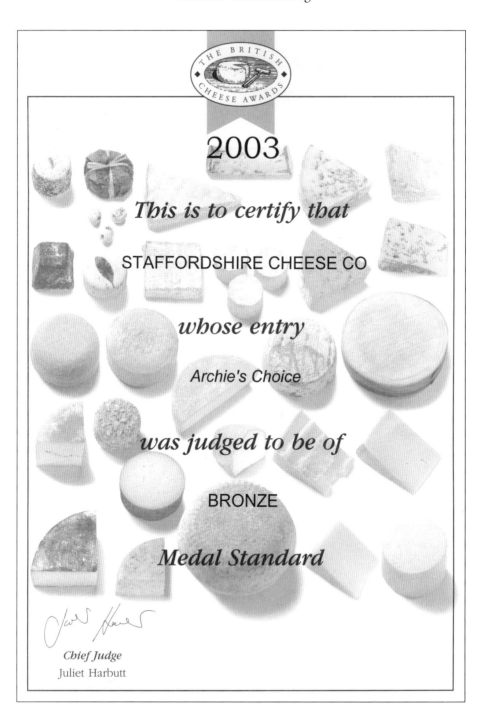

THE BRITISH CHEESE AWARDS

2003

This is to certify that

STAFFORDSHIRE CHEESE CO

whose entry

Archie's Choice

was judged to be of

BRONZE

Medal Standard

Chief Judge
Juliet Harbutt

THE BRITISH CHEESE AWARDS

2003

This is to certify that

STAFFORDSHIRE CHEESE CO

whose entry

Rudyard

was judged to be of

BRONZE

Medal Standard

Chief Judge
Juliet Harbutt

Est 1819
BAKEWELL SHOW
Main Sponsors
GORDON LAMB

BAKEWELL
AGRICULTURAL
& HORTICULTURAL
SOCIETY LTD.

CHEESE COMPETITION

FIRST PRIZE

presented to

John Knox Ltd.

for

Class C.6. Single Crumbly   *Bakewell Show* 1998

Edwin .... Referee   Linda Taylor .... Manager

Date .... 5ᵗ August

Dairy Farmers of Britain ®

12 March 2004

Mr J Knox
Staffordshire Cheese Co Ltd.
Glenmore House
55 Rose Bank
Leek
Staffordshire
ST13 6AG

Dear John,

RE: Milk Deliveries

With reference to your recent enquiry regarding the milk deliveries made to your
site by Dairy Farmers of Britain. I am pleased to confirm that all milk, forming
these deliveries, is collected from farms within the county of Staffordshire.

I trust this clarifies the position, however should you require any further
information please do not hesitate to contact me again.

Yours sincerely,

J A Horton (Mrs)
Quality & Account Manager

Appendix 11

Cheese yields

Much has been written concerning yields of cheese from a given volume of milk. Various formulae have been reported from time to time for the calculation of the yields of hard or semi-hard cheese from milk.

The accuracy of these formulae depends on the analytical and sampling methods. These formulae do not take account of the milk constituents lost in the whey and, therefore, the methods of manufacture, the type of cheese and the ripening of the cheese may cause the formulae to be misleading.

The ratio of cheese sold agist milk used is a more realistic exercise. In territorial cheese manufacture yields of 9.3 litres of milk per kilogram of cheese and 8.93 litres of milk per kilogram of cheese have been observed.

Hard cheese made from full cream milk has a legal 48% fat in the dry matter and not more than 40% water.

Exceptions:

Derby, Leicester, Blue Stilton not more than 42% water

Cheshire, Gloucester, Double Gloucester not more than 44% water

Caerphilly, Wensleydale, White Stilton not more than 46% water

Lancashire not more than 48% water

All of the above cheeses obviously give a better yield than, say Cheddar.

Soft Cheese: Full fat cheese not less than 20% fat or more than 60% water

Medium fat cheese, not less than 20% fat or more than 70% water

Skimmed milk cheese, not less than 2% fat or more than 80% water

Scott (Cheesemaking Practice) states that to produce cheeses of quality in body and texure the casein / fat ratio has to be in the range 0.69 to 0.71:1. Normally artisanal cheeses are made directly from the milk available without attempting to standardise.

The type of cheese made will have a major impact on your cash flow and the amount of cheese you make:

- Soft cheeses like Brie and Camembert and fresh cheese like cream cheese or curd cheese have relatively short shelf lives and must be made and sold within weeks of being made. The benefit of this is that you get your money back quickly. The downside is that levels of wastage can be higher. These cheeses have relatively high levels of moisture and therefore the yield from a given amount of milk will be much better than those on hard cheeses. For example, 100 litres of milk will yield perhaps 14 kgs of Camembert.

- Hard and semi-hard cheeses like Cheddar, Cheshire, Red Leicester or Lancashire have potentially long shelf lives but can take months to mature. Wastage levels may therefore be lower as ripening times can be regulated by controlling the storage temperature. However, as the moisture levels in these cheeses is much lower than in soft and fresh cheeses, yields from a given amount of milk are much lower. For example, 100 litres of milk will yield about 10 kgs of Cheddar.

Training

All cheese staff must be suitably trained to ensure product quality and safety. Regular cheese courses are run at Reaseheath College, but cheesemaking staff must also be train on-site and training records kept.

Index